# MUSICIANS·INSTITUTE

# Guitar Soloing

### by Daniel Gilbert and Beth Marlis

ISBN 0-7935-8186-9

# HAL·LEONARD®
## CORPORATION

7777 W. BLUEMOUND RD. P.O. BOX 13819 MILWAUKEE, WI 53213

Visit Hal Leonard Online at
**www.halleonard.com**

# About the Authors

**D**aniel Gilbert is a New York City-born guitarist who has been working at Musicians Institute since 1979. He has written much of the school's guitar-based curriculum, including *Single String Improvisation, Funk Rhythm Guitar, and Applied Technique.*

Along with his busy recording schedule, Daniel continues to do club gigs, sessions, and seminars in California, as well as Japan, the East Coast, and Europe. Daniel is currently working on his second album of rock, jazz, and blues based instrumental music. (His first album, *Mr. Invisable,* is distributed in Europe.)

**B**eth Marlis has been an Instructor at Musicians Institute since 1987. She teaches Single String Improvisation, Music Reading, Rhythm Guitar, Music History, and Open Counseling.

While working her way up the musical food chain, she received a Master of Music degree from U.S.C., and performed with a wide range of artists including Harold Land, Brownie McGee, Louis Bellson, Helen Reddy, et al. She has also been involved with various music videos, studio recording projects and film, while maintaining a career as a professional "sideman" in Los Angeles.

# Table of Contents

# Introduction

**T**his book is a guide to learning and mastering the craft of guitar improvisation in popular music. Two of M.I.'s top instructors lay out a comprehensive, step-by-step approach to developing the chops and musicianship to help you play professional quality solos in any style. Each chapter gives you diagrams, exercises, techniques, licks, and an "insider's view" on how to apply each and every sound. The play along CD is packed with great grooves to help you practice applying the conceps presented. Also included are 36 licks—one at the start of each track.

This book will provide you with a solid foundation for understanding and *using* the fretboard creatively! Take your time and play it through from cover to cover, or work on each chapter as needed.

Enjoy and happy soloing!

# Practice Tips

**Y**ou will need to find the "right place" for your daily practicing. The important ingredients of a good practice environment are:

a)   A comfortable chair, to help you keep good posture (Do not hunch over your guitar!). You need to be able to stay relaxed and focused. You may want to practice in a standing position (to simulate a typical performance experience).

b)   A quiet place where you will not be disturbed (this is sometimes difficult!).

c)   A desk, music stand, or tabletop that is uncluttered (at the right height) for you to easily access this book, a metronome (or drum machine/sequencer), paper, and a tape recorder.

d)   Good lighting is also important to eliminate eye strain and fatigue.

e)   This is your laboratory!

While it may not always be possible for you to practice in your "ultimate practice spot," you should make an attempt to find these elements wherever you practice.

# Getting Started

**1**

## Objectives

- To give guidelines for positioning of fretting and picking hands.

- To play basic right and left hand coordination exercises with alternate picking.

- To begin an understanding of the "layout" of the fingerboard.

- To play a one octave major scale in any key using a pattern whose tonic is located on the sixth and fourth, or fifth and third strings.

- To play the notes of the scales over a chord progression in a major key using quarter- and eighth-note rhythms.

### EXERCISE 1: Stretching Exercise

It is very important that we always start off our practice time with some warm-up and stretching exercises. The purpose of these exercises is to insure that our playing is relaxed, natural, and not stressful to our muscles and joints. As we continue through this book, various warm-up exercises will be suggested. Let's start out with a good basic loosening-up movement that will improve blood circulation and muscle relaxation.

Sit (or stand) comfortably. Raise both hands above your head and shake them strongly for 10-20 seconds; let them drop down to your side. You should feel the blood rushing into your fingertips. Repeat.

## Fret-Hand Positioning

Place your hand so that you have one finger per fret on the low E string in first position *(position refers to the fret at which your index finger is located.)* The ball of your thumb should contact the middle of the neck approximately beneath your second finger. The angle of your wrist to your arm should be natural. Arch your fingers out over the fingerboard. When any finger is not actually fretting a note, keep it as close to the fingerboard as possible (roughly 1/8" to 1/2" above the strings).

## Pick-Hand Positioning

Hold the pick firmly between the thumb and the first finger. The fingers and palm of your hand can be loosely cupped. Your wrist should float smoothly above the bridge. (A light brushing against the bridge is acceptable as long as the wrist is not "nailed" to the bridge in any one location.) *There should be no excess tension anywhere in your picking hand, wrist, or arm!*

## Positioning of the Pick and Note Execution

Angling the pick slightly downward helps produce a good sound and allows the pick to slide off the string in preparation for the next picking action. The motion for each stroke comes from the wrist and hand. During the actual stroke, the pick should remain close to the strings. Keep the pick stroke short, yet use enough energy to produce a strong sound. There should be as little vertical motion (away from the face of the guitar) as possible.

These are guidelines meant to give you a starting point in getting a good sound. There are many guitar techniques which will require you to alter the guidelines on the previous page to achieve a certain sound or affect. Many great players have very different approaches. However, using the positioning and basic note execution guidelines described here will develop an efficient and versatile approach to the instrument.

# Methods of Notation

To get the student understanding and playing these exercises as quickly as possible, this book will use three methods of notating exercises. The first will use *standard musical notation* combined with fingerings and string markings, the second will use a system called *tablature,* and the third will use *fretboard diagrams* accompanied by an explanation on how to play the presented material. The following is a brief description of the second and third methods described above.

## *Tablature*

*Tablature* is a system of music notation developed specifically for guitarists. It takes place on a six-line staff, each line representing one of the six strings of the guitar. The number indicates the fret and string location on the guitar where the note is to be played. Tablature is a very incomplete system of music notation. Always refer to the music notation staff for right and left hand fingerings, rhythmic notation, or any other necessary information.

**Fig. 1**

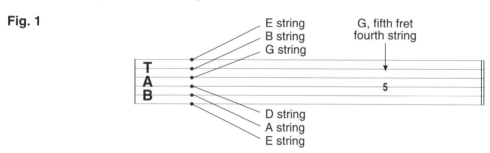

## *Horizontal Fretboard Diagrams*

*Horizontal fretboard diagrams* show the neck of the guitar from the first fret to the twelfth fret. The parallel lines represent the strings and the vertical lines represent the frets. The dots will represent string and fret locations where notes are to be played. The open dots represent standard fretboard inlays that will help you quickly find the correct position.

**Fig. 2**

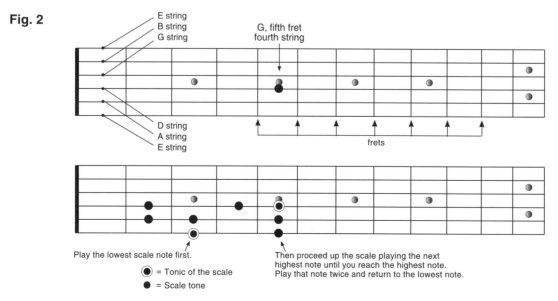

# Using a Metronome

A *metronome* (and/or a drum machine/sequencer) is one of the most important tools an aspiring musician owns. All exercises should be practiced with a metronome and an awareness of the tempo and rhythms you are working with. In the early stages, play quarter notes (that is, playing a note for each click of the metronome) moving gradually toward using other sub-divisions of the beat (eighth notes are two note attacks per beat of the metronome; sixteenth notes, four attacks; triplets, three attacks; etc.). There are many other techniques for practicing with the metronome.

# Alternate Picking

There are many possible ways to pick a given phrase. This book will introduce the guitarist to all of them. In the beginning stages *alternate picking* (consecutive down and upstrokes) is the most effective method. The student should pay attention to making the upstroke (an inherently weaker attack) sound the same as a downstroke. Unless other instructions are given, the student should use alternate picking.

# Basic Exercises

The following exercises help coordinate the fretting and picking hands. Perform them utilizing the guidelines given previously. Strive to produce a full sound.

**EXERCISE 2: Technique Exercise**

**EXERCISE 3: Technique Exercise**

These are variations focusing on the picking hand. Continue alternate picking throughout these exercises.

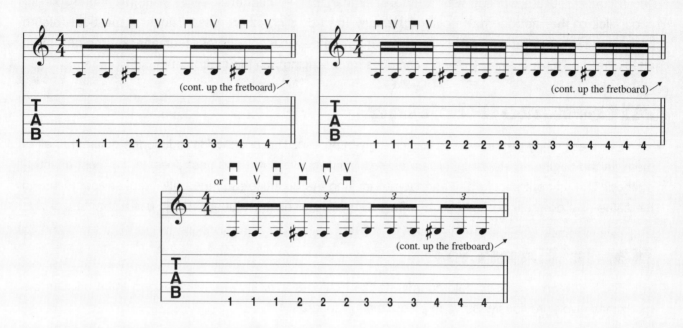

These exercises are meant to help coordinate the hands and build finger dexterity, though they sometimes can be used as a source of melodic material.

# The "Layout" of the Fingerboard

There are many approaches to playing scales and other melodic devices on the guitar. The system we will use is based on five patterns (the pattern is the overall "shape" of the scale or arpeggio). These one-octave patterns are closely related to the five open position chords (C, A, G, E, and D). Variations of this approach will be discussed after a solid grounding in these patterns has been established.

**Fig. 3**

Pattern 1 is built around the C chord:

Pattern 2 is built around the A chord:

Pattern 3 is built around the G chord:

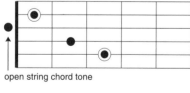

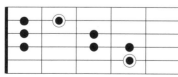
open string chord tone

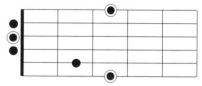

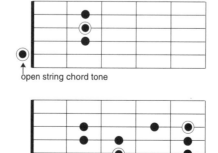
open string chord tone

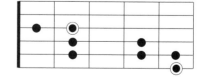

Pattern 4 is built around the E chord:                   Pattern 5 is built around the D chord:

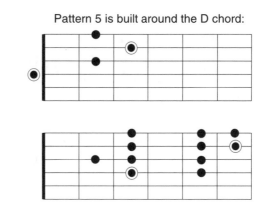

# Single String/Improv

When these patterns are laid *end to end* they give the guitarist a picture of *one key* up and down the fingerboard. When these patterns are superimposed over each other in *the same position* they yield *five different keys*. This idea will be stressed throughout the book.

We will be learning pieces of these patterns and then begin building the entire pattern, joining all the patterns together to form a complete command of the fingerboard. Remember the long term goal is to *make music* using all melodic devices in any key anywhere on the fingerboard. The short term (daily) goal is to make music with whatever patterns one knows *now!*

# Playing Moveable Major Scale Patterns

All the patterns we will be learning are "moveable." Moving a *pattern* to a different *position* yields a different *key*. To play any of the patterns in a given key, shift the position of the pattern so the circled note(s) in the diagram are over the intended tonic.

We will begin by looking at a one-octave major scale pattern. This pattern forms the lower octave of pattern 4.

**Fig. 4: pattern 4**

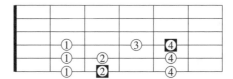

Play this pattern in the key of G major by placing your fretting hand in second position and spreading out the fingers in a one-finger-per-fret "stance." Using the fingerings given above, play the scale starting on the lowest tonic, up to the highest note in the pattern (G in this instance). Play that note twice and then back down to the lowest note. Use alternate picking.

Now, look at the lower octave of pattern 2.

**Fig. 5: pattern 2**

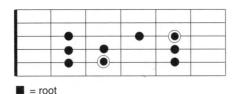

■ = root

Notice that it has exactly the same shape and fingering as the lower octave of pattern 4, except that its tonics are located on the fifth and third strings. Play this scale pattern in the key of G also. Do this by moving the pattern up the neck until the circled notes are over the G notes on the fifth and third strings. This puts your hand in the ninth position. Play this scale using the exact same method used in the previous pattern 4 example (highest note twice, alternative picking).

# Using the Major Scale

The use of melodic devices (scales just being one of them) is tied to the harmony of whatever music you are playing. For now, this book will utilize the harmonies of the major scale (referred to as major tonality)—specifically the chords built on the first, fourth, and fifth degrees of the major scale. These are referred to as the I, IV, and V chords and in major tonality each of them is major. The play-a-long CD that accompanies this book contains progressions with the I, IV, and V chords in different keys and rhythmic styles for you to practice with. It is critical that you use the play-a-long CD to familiarize your ear with note choices that fit the harmonies of the given progression!

**Chapter 1 Lick**

Play this lick over the Chapter 1 chord progression (see next page).

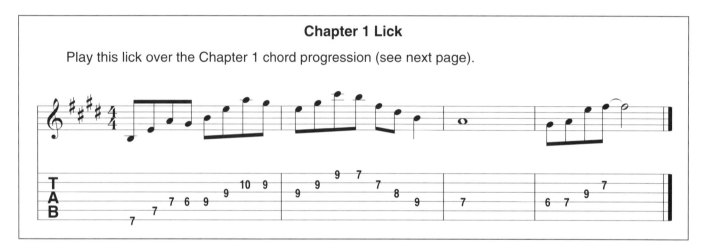

**1 Chapter 1 Chord Progression**

This progression in E major uses the I, IV, and V chords. Play the new major scale patterns you've learned along with the accompanying CD track.

It's time for you to "go for it!" Play in the key of E major, using both patterns, trying different rhythms (like eighth notes, sixteenth notes, triplets, rests, quarter notes, etc.)! Don't always play the same rhythms, or order of notes. Try to make short, melodic sounding ideas. Have fun; you can do "no wrong" as long as you stay with your major scale shapes.

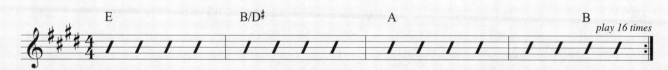

As the CD plays, try playing both patterns of the E major scale over the rhythm track. Hold each note of the scale for long durations (sustained notes such as whole notes). Listen to the sound and color of each tone against the chord progression; make note of what sounds good to you. Pay attention to how the notes might sound good together, in what order, etc. Do not play fast! Listen!

- Creativity suggestions:

  1. Sing any short melody or lick, and try to copy it on your guitar (find the sounds). Try this with "easy songs" like nursery rhymes, too.

  2. Try starting exercises #1, 2, 3 in the middle of the exercise, or at the end!

  3. Wherever you hear music playing, or being practiced, try to notice if the melody (or solo) uses the sounds of the major scale.

- Visualization suggestions:

  1. "Play" all of your new exercises on your arm! (no guitar). Do it as "air guitar," too. Try tapping out new fingering patterns on a tabletop.

  2. "See" yourself playing your "dream gig," with your favorite band, favorite guitar, favorite venue, and playing great!

  3. Before going to sleep at night, review/remember your best musical moments of the day.

| Chapter One | REVIEW |
|---|---|

1. Understand and begin using the pointers for hand positioning.

2. Play basic exercises from this chapter.

3. Be able to play a one-octave major scale up and down in any key using the lower octave of patterns 2 and 4.

4. Be able to play over the given progression using a combination of whole, half, and quarter rhythms.

# Major Scales and Sequencing

## 2

## Objectives

- Learn to play the upper octaves of patterns 2 and 4.

- Understand the concept of diatonic scale sequencing.

- Learn to play two sequences in the major scale using patterns 2 and 4.

- Use the diatonic sequences and the full two-octave scale patterns over a major tonality chord progression.

- Use quarter and eighth-note rhythms to improvise melodies over the given progression.

### EXERCISE 1 – Technique Exercise

This technique exercise consists of variations on Chapter 1's technique exercise (1-2-3-4 fingering combination). Its purpose is to build dexterity, synchronization, and accuracy of technique. There will be many other variations in upcoming chapters.

a) Going "up" (ascending) play: 1-3-2-4 fingering; (descending) play: 4-2-3-1.

b) (Ascending) play: 2-1-3-4; (descending) play: 4-3-1-2.

## Major Scale Patterns

We will continue working with the major scale by learning to play the upper octaves of patterns 2 and 4. Look at the upper octave of pattern 4:

**Fig. 1: major scale pattern 4**

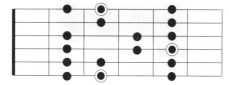 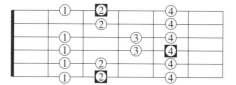

Notice that this upper octave extends one note beyond the tonic. (One note below the lowest tonic has also been added). The patterns we will be working with frequently contain notes higher and lower than the tonic. Now look at the upper octave of pattern 2:

**Fig. 2: major scale pattern 2**

 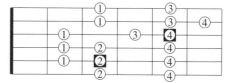

This pattern does not extend a full two octaves. Pattern 2 also contains notes lower than the lowest tonic.

Practice each of these patterns starting on the lowest tonic, playing up to the highest note in the pattern (which may or may not be the tonic) then down to the lowest note and back up to the lowest tonic. This gives the guitarist the full range of notes in the given pattern and key. Practice these two patterns in all keys.

## EXERCISE 2

Play two-octave shapes of major scale patterns 4 and 2 in the suggested keys, using eighth notes and alternate picking. Start and end each pattern on the tonic.

Variations:

a) Use 2 attacks (eighth notes) per scale step (play each note two times for each metronome click).

b) Use 3 attacks per scale step (play each note three times per click; this creates a triplet rhythm).

# Diatonic Scale Sequencing

Obviously, the major scale is not just played up and down. The guitarist must learn methods of manipulating the notes of these scales (or any scale for that matter) to produce melodies. Besides using your ear, one method players use is *diatonic scale sequencing*. *Diatonic* means "using only the notes of the scale," and *sequencing* can be described as "an arrangement of scale pitches whose relationships are repeated on each step of the scale." If we number the notes of a scale from 1 to 8, with 1 being the tonic and 8 representing the next higher tonic, diatonic sequences could be represented as: 1-2-3-4, 2-3-4-5, 3-4-5-6, etc. We will call this the "groups of four" sequence. When playing one of these, continue the sequence up to the highest pitch within the scale pattern, then reverse the sequence and play it back down the scale. (The descending line is 8-7-6-5, 7-6-5-4, 6-5-4-3, etc.)

Scale sequencing is an important aspect of single note playing. It does several things:

1. Familiarizes the guitarist with the scale patterns
2. Exercises the fingers
3. Provides the guitarist with material to develop melodic motifs
4. "Educates" the ears so the player can more easily "hear" what other players are doing.

There are an unlimited amount of scale sequencing ideas. Again, these exercises give the guitarist material to help construct melodies and the more of these one knows, the better. This is an ongoing process and should be viewed as just one of the things you practice. The next figure demonstrates the groups of four sequence, ascending and descending in one octave of the major scale.

**Fig. 3: "group of four" sequence in pattern #4**

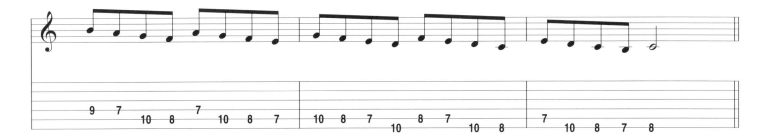

Using alternate picking, apply this sequence to the full range of notes in pattern 4, then in pattern 2. Practice this in different keys.

Note: Fingerings will be dictated by the scale pattern you're playing that sequence in. Different sequences will require slight alterations of the fingerings in these patterns. Use the fingering comfortable for you and remain as close as possible to the pattern shape and position you are in.

This next sequence is called "diatonic thirds." The formula for this sequence would be 1-3, 2-4, 3-5; descending 8-6, 7-5, etc. The intervals are a combination of major and minor thirds. The next figure demonstrates this in a one-octave scale pattern ascending and descending:

**Fig. 4: "diatonic thirds" sequence in pattern #2**

Apply this sequence to the full range of notes in patterns 4 and 2. Practice this in different keys. Continue using alternate picking for these exercises even though you are crossing strings. This helps to build dexterity in the picking hand.

# Combining Scale Sequences over a Major Chord Progression

Now try mixing up pieces of the sequences to produce something like this:

**Fig. 5**

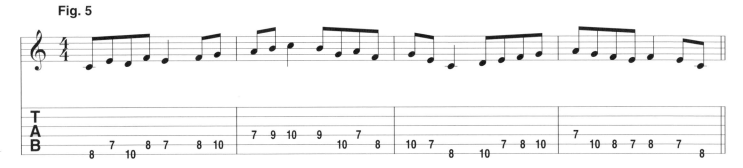

Try this on your own at a slow tempo. To help transition from one sequence to the next, use a half (or quarter) note, picking up with a new sequence in eighth notes.

Play the suggested progression at the end of this chapter and try switching sequences. Use eighth notes and the method described above.

# Using Quarter- and Eighth-Note Rhythms

Steady eight-, triplet-, or sixteenth-note rhythms are very useful for training the hands and ears, but music combines sound and silence to create interest. This means combining different rhythms with rests. Read the following rhythmic example and be able to clap and sing it. Practice choosing notes from the scale and applying the rhythm to them, like so:

**Fig. 6**

This is a rudimentary exercise aimed at making the student more aware of rhythms. Play along with the following progression and apply different rhythms to your note choices.

There is more to music than just combining notes and rhythms over a chord progression. These methods are intended to move the student toward developing a better "ear." There will be more on this in upcoming chapters.

### Chapter 2 Lick

Use this lick over the Chapter 2 chord progression.

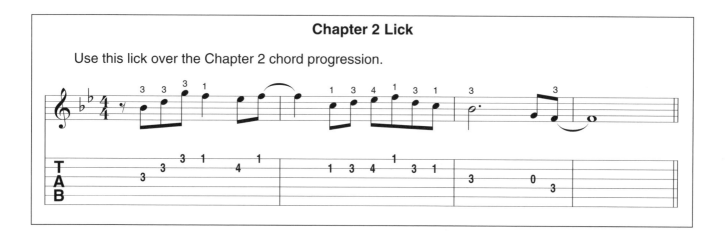

### 2 Chapter 2 Chord Progression

This is a I-IV-V progression in B♭ major.

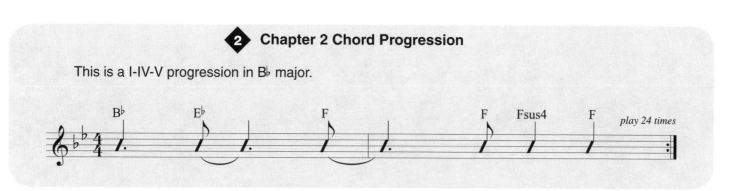

## EXERCISE 3

Play scale sequences for patterns 4 and 2 in two octaves. Use only eighth notes and alternate picking. Listen to the fragments or melodic building blocks that are created by your sequencing.

| Chapter Two | REVIEW |
|---|---|

1.  Be able to play the full two-octave patterns 4 and 2 in any key.

2.  Be able to play the "groups of four" and "diatonic thirds" sequences ascending and descending in patterns 4 and 2 in any key.

3.  Be able to understand and apply new scale sequences to the major scale patterns.

4.  Be able to combine sequences and rhythms over the given major tonality chord progression.

# Major Scales and Arpeggios

## Objectives

- Present remaining patterns with an explanation of long and short term goals in learning all the material.

- Learn to arpeggiate the triad shapes of the I, IV, and V chords in patterns 2 and 4.

- Combine scale and arpeggio movement.

- Introduce hammer-ons and pull-offs.

- Combine hammer-ons and pull-offs with all previous material over a major tonality chord progression.

---

**EXERCISE 1 – Stretching Exercise**

Grab onto your own wrist. With the "free" hand, make a fist (not too tightly) gently rotate it in a "clockwise" motion, then reverse directions. Change over to the other wrist, and repeat the same motions. This exercise will help to "loosen" the wrist joints.

---

## Major Scale Patterns, Long and Short Term Goals

The next figure gives fretboard and fingering diagrams for the major scale patterns 1, 3, and 5.

**Fig. 1**

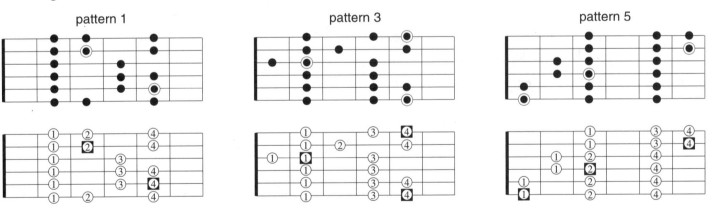

These patterns give the student a complete picture of the five patterns based on the open position chords in Chapter 1. The student should learn and drill these patterns only after patterns 2 and 4 have been memorized and are available for immediate recall to make melodies in any major key. This may take some time depending on the starting point of each student. This is *fine!* It is more desirable to know two patterns and be able to use them, than to be unsure and unable to use all five. Your long term goal is to be able to play music using all devices (scales, arpeggios, etc.), in any key, anywhere on the neck. Your short term goal is to make music with all the devices you know now, in any key, in two places on the neck.

# Arpeggio Shapes for the I, IV, and V Chords

So far we have only used the major scale. Let's begin looking at arpeggio playing. *Arpeggios* are the tones of a chord played as single notes. They can be used to spell out the sound of a chord, or to create melodic interest. We will learn to arpeggiate the I, IV, and V chords of the major scale. These are called *triads* because they contain the three pitches (root, third, and fifth) needed to define a chord. Look at the shape of each of these triad arpeggios in the lower octave of pattern 4:

**Fig. 2: pattern 4 lower octave**

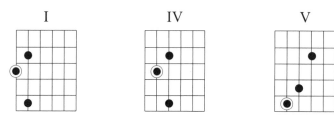

Practice each of these shapes ascending and descending. The same arpeggios can be found in the upper octave of pattern 4 as well, though their shapes are different:

**Fig. 3: pattern 4 upper octave**

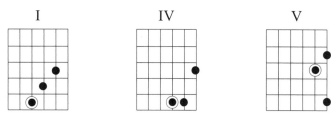

Now look at the I, IV, and V triad arpeggios in the lower octave of pattern 2. Practice each of these shapes ascending and descending.

**Fig. 4: pattern 2 lower octave**

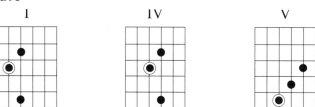

# Combining Scale and Arpeggios Movement

Did you notice the different intervals that arpeggios make you play? The arpeggios use a combination of major and minor thirds. This may challenge your picking hand, but for the moment use alternate picking. The following exercise combines the triad arpeggios with scale movement in pattern 4, key of C:

**EXERCISE 2**

Make up your own studies that mix up the arpeggios with scale movement. Try to hear the different effect of the I, IV, and V chords. Does this remind you of any songs you've heard? It should, as there are literally thousands of songs based on these three chords. Put on the play-a-long progression (track 3) and improvise. Play the IV chord arpeggios when you hear it in the progression. Try this with the I and V chords as well. Mix this up with scale motion.

# Hammer-ons and Pull-offs

Up to this point, alternate picking has been used exclusively. Let's look at another way of producing notes: hammer-ons and pull-offs.

Hammer-ons are executed by sounding a note with a down or upstroke, then snapping a different finger down on a higher note on the same string. This is notated using a slur marking between the two notes:

**Fig. 5: hammer-ons**

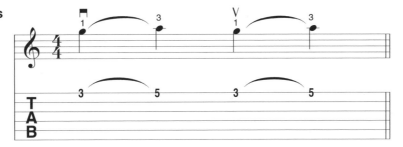

Pull-offs are the opposite. Pick a note and snap off its finger to a lower note on the same string. This action is notated in the same fashion as above:

**Fig. 6: pull-offs**

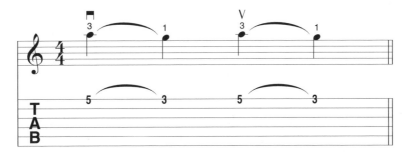

These movements need to be performed with some extra energy in order to produce a strong sound. They are very natural actions and very important ones as they give the notes a different sound and give the guitarist the ability to play several notes with only one pick attack. The tone is a smoother one when these actions are used—not as sharp as an ordinary pick stroke. The following exercises are good for practicing hammer-ons and pull-offs and also demonstrate sounding more than one note with a single pick stroke. Practice these on each string as well as moving them chromatically (up and down each string).

Use the suggested play-a-long progressions to practice combining everything presented in this chapter.

**EXERCISE 2**

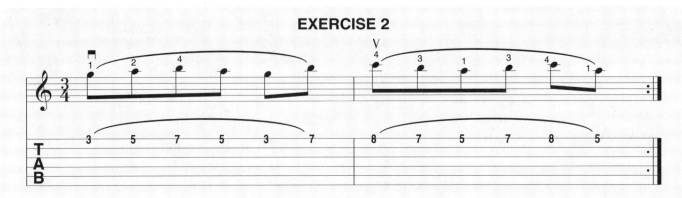

Play both of these exercises on all strings, in different positions, or moving them chromatically.

**EXERCISE 3**

## Chapter 3 Lick

This lick uses hammer-on and pull-off ideas. Try it over the Chapter 3 chord progression.

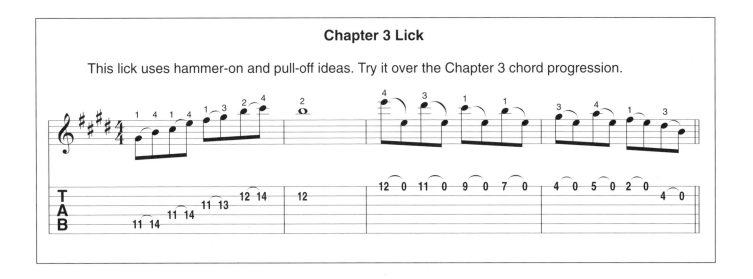

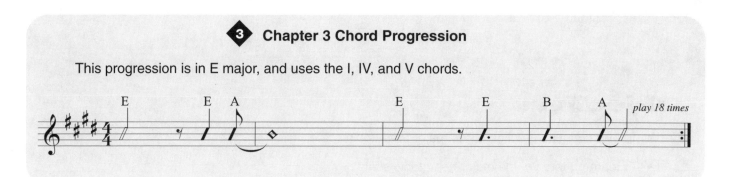

**3** **Chapter 3 Chord Progression**

This progression is in E major, and uses the I, IV, and V chords.

| Chapter Three | **REVIEW** |
|---|---|

1. Understand long and short term goals for learning all the major scale patterns.

2. Be able to arpeggiate the I, IV, and V chord triads in two patterns in any key.

3. Be able to combine scale and arpeggio movement over a major tonality chord progression.

4. Be able to apply hammer-ons and pull-offs to major tonality improvising.

# The Major Pentatonic Scale

**4**

## Objectives

- To learn the construction of the major pentatonic scale.

- To learn patterns of the major pentatonic scale.

- To apply sequences to the major pentatonic scale.

- To combine the major scale and the pentatonic scale.

- To learn how to play with a distorted tone.

### EXERCISE 1: Technique Exercise

This technique exercise uses a 1-2-3-4 fingering (like our original exercise in Chapter 1), but with a slight twist to it! You are still playing a 1-2-3-4 fingering, but now you alternate strings! It ends up looking like a zig-zag shape.

## Major Pentatonic Scale

*Pentatonic scales,* in may forms, are found all over the world. They are one of the most basic sounds in music, and are found in many cultures.

The *major pentatonic scale* contains five pitches. It can be viewed as a major scale with the fourth and seventh degrees left out. From a tonic of C, this gives the following notes:

| C | D | E | G | A | C |
|---|---|---|---|---|---|
| 1 | 2 | 3 | 5 | 6 | 1(8) |

The scale's construction yields notes a minor third apart (E to G, and A up to C). This gives the pentatonic scale an "open" sound. The sound of the major pentatonic is quite distinctive, and is most readily associated with country music, though it can be found in blues, rock, and jazz. Be able to construct a major pentatonic scale from any tonic. Again, this can be done by leaving the fourth and seventh degrees out of the major scale from the desired tonic.

# Patterns of the Major Pentatonic Scale

Patterns of this scale are derived from the major scale patterns. As a matter of fact, *any new scale in the major tonality will be presented as a variation of the major scale.* The following are two patterns for the major pentatonic scale (patterns 2 and 4):

**Fig. 1**

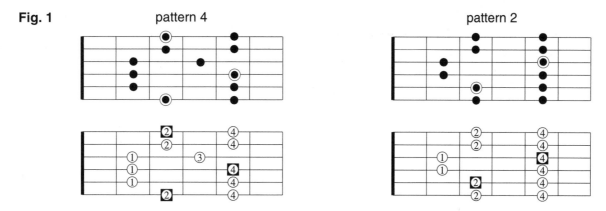

## EXERCISE 2

Play pattern 4 of the major pentatonic scale in eighth notes (or triplets) in the key of G. Next, play pattern 2 in the key of G as well (the same tonic). You should have found yourself at the second fret for pattern 4 and at the ninth fret for pattern 2.

Now you should be able to play these two patterns of the major pentatonic scale, ascending and descending, in any key.

# Sequencing the Major Pentatonic Scale

Again, let's begin playing melodies by trying some sequences. The next figure demonstrates the "group of four" sequence, but using the notes of the major pentatonic only:

**Fig. 2: major pentatonic "groups of four" sequence**

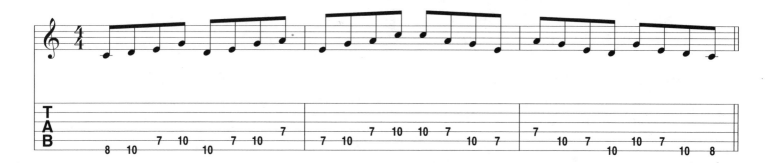

Of course, other sequences are possible. The following figure demonstrates the ascending and descending versions of several sequences. Apply each of these to the entire range of notes in two patterns of the major pentatonic scale.

**Fig. 3: major pentatonic sequences**

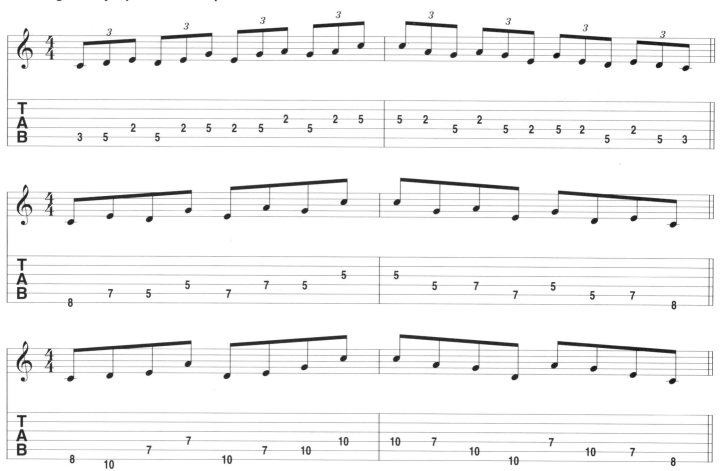

Sometimes these sequences force the player to alter the fingering of the pattern—that's fine. Simply stay in the overall shape of the pattern. The picking hand should be able to alternate pick these sequences but also practice them using hammer-ons and pull-offs.

## EXERCISE 3

In the key of G, play patterns 4 and 2 with a "group of four sequence" in eighth notes.

Now, apply the three newly furnished scale sequences to both patterns of the major pentatonic scale in the key of G. This process will certainly take some practice, because you are learning new sequences and trying them in a new scale!

Remember that the major pentatonic should feel familiar to your fingers because it is based on the major scale shapes. Be aware that the major pentatonic has a distinct flavor and tonal character that is different from the major scale.

# Combining the Major and Major Pentatonic Scales

As stated earlier, the major pentatonic may be viewed as the major scale with the fourth and seventh degrees omitted. Combining notes from the major scale and major pentatonic from the same tonic can add some variation to your melodies. Ultimately, you want to hear pentatonic melodies and combine them with melodies drawn from the major scale. Until these sounds can really be heard we can use these technical devices to assist us. First, try *ascending the major scale and descending the major pentatonic:*

**Fig. 4**

Now reverse it:

**Fig. 5**

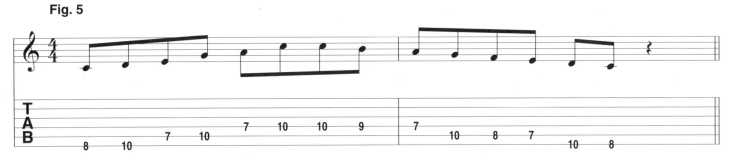

This next figure combines two different sequences and the two scales. Again, these are just devices to assist you in hearing each of these scales and combining them to make melodies.

**Fig. 6**

# Playing with a Distorted Tone

The era of modern electronics has allowed the guitarist to achieve many different sounds. Reverb, echo, flanging, pitch shifting, and many other effects are all important facets of a guitarist's sound. One of the most important effects the modern guitarist is called on to use is a *distorted* sound. This may be achieved either through the amplifier itself or a separate unit. These all work in a similar fashion: by overdriving the pre-amplifier stage of the amp or the use of an add-on device. The focus of this discussion is the physical techniques needed to execute these sounds cleanly.

## *Picking Hand*

A distorted sound is generally a loud one (or at least designed to sound loud) with a lot of sustain. To control other strings from ringing and producing extraneous sounds, the palm of the picking hand is used to mute the string. The palm may move across the bridge as the higher strings are played. The key here is to control the amount of string vibration without losing too much of the main tone. This is very much a "feel" thing. Play up and down the major pentatonic scale using varying degrees of muting. Try this with both a clean and dirty tone.

## *Fretting Hand*

The fretting hand can also assist in the muting of notes by lifting up the finger after the desired sustain of the note is achieved. In addition, parts of other fingers that are not fretting a note may be used to help mute non-essential strings. The outer edge of the fourth finger, and the pads of the other fingers may be used. Again, the player must get a "feel" for how much muting, when, etc...These muting techniques are very important for controlling the distorted tone. Later, they will be combined with bending techniques to give the guitarist the ability to execute modern guitar techniques cleanly. Practice muting techniques with a clean and a dirty tone while playing over the following progressions on the play-a-long CD.

### Chapter 4: Lick

This swinging eighth-note lick is based on a G major pentatonic scale with a B♭ passing tone. Try this lick over the chapter 4 chord progression.

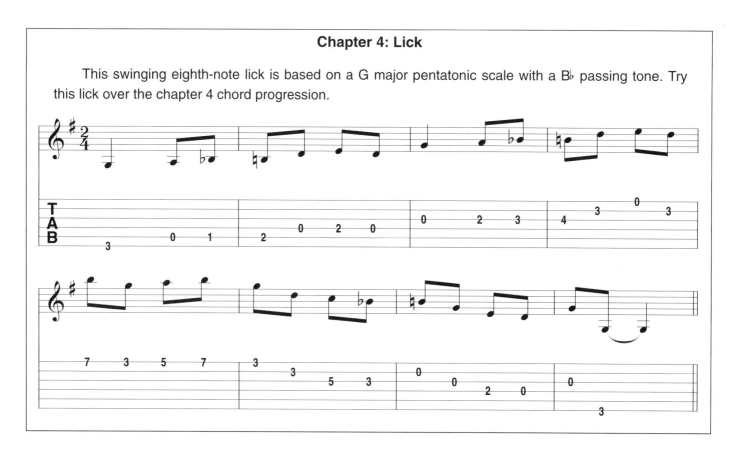

### Chapter 4: Chord Progression

This is an uptempo "two-beat" progression. Hint: you do not need to play a fast solo in this case; pay attention to making satisfying musical ideas with the major pentatonic scale and/or its sequences! This G major progression uses the I, IV, and V chords.

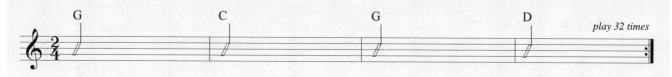

| Chapter Four | **REVIEW** |
|---|---|

1. Be able to construct a major pentatonic scale from any tonic.

2. Be able to play two patterns of the major pentatonic in any key.

3. Be able to play two sequences ascending and descending through the entire range of two patterns of the major pentatonic scale.

4. Be able to mix up motion from the major and major pentatonic scales.

5. Begin using muting from both hands to produce notes cleanly with a distorted tone.

6. Be able to combine all these devices over the play-a-long progression.

# Major Pentatonic Scales and Bends

**5**

## Objectives

- Present remaining patterns of the major pentatonic scale.
- Techniques and exercises using bends.
- Combining bends and major tonality scales over major chord progressions.

### Exercise 1: Visualization Exercise

Visualize any pattern of the major scale on your instrument. For example, you might want to "see" pattern 4 of the A major scale. Can you picture the next pattern above or below it? Since you are in fifth position to begin with, can you "see" pattern 3 of A major (covers the second-fifth frets); or can you "see" pattern 5 (fifth-tenth frets)? You might want to look at diagrams of these patterns, play them and then try to visualize them. If you are able to do this without too much difficulty, try to picture the entire neck in all five patterns of the A major scale (laid end to end)! Try this in different keys, too.

## Patterns of the Major Pentatonic Scale

Here are the remaining patterns of the major pentatonic scale (patterns 1, 3, and 5):

**Fig. 1**

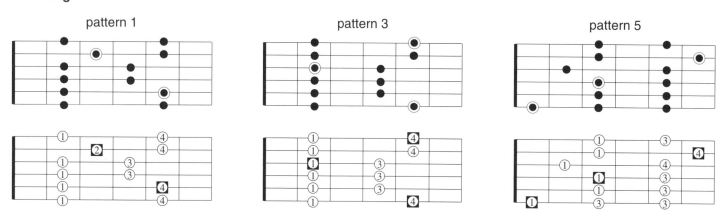

Remember the long and short term goals discussed in Chapter 3. Work on these patterns only after patterns 2 and 4 are available for immediate recall and use. If you are ready to learn and use these new patterns, apply sequences and play them in all keys. You can also use them to improvise over the play-a-long progressions.

## Techniques and Exercises for the Use of Bends

*Bending* is one of the most expressive devices available to the guitarist. It is a widely used technique in many styles—most notably blues and rock. Bending requires the guitarist to develop some different techniques. The first, and most important, technical point about bending is the thumb of the fretting hand. To give the fingers an "anchor" for the bending finger to push against, the thumb must be brought over the top of the fretboard. This is a departure from the technique guidelines given in Chapter

1, but as was stated then, these guidelines are often broken to achieve a certain sound. "Hook" the thumb over the top edge of the fingerboard. The finger is actually moving the string. However, a lot of players move their wrist towards the fingerboard which in turn moves the finger to bend the note. Ultimately the player should be able to bend with every finger, but for now, concentrate on the first and third fingers. Place your third finger on the second string at the eighth fret (a G note). Push the string towards your thumb. Make sure you get enough of the tip of your finger underneath the note so it feels secure enough that the string doesn't slide out from underneath the finger (a very common problem). While you are doing this, listen! Try bending the note a whole step up. You should hear an A note. This is one of the most difficult aspects of bending—intonation. Let's look at how this would be notated:

**Fig. 2**

Bends are notated with an arrow in the TAB *above the note you are bending,* not the note you are bending to! In the notation, a "pointed slur" joins the note you are bending from to the note you are bending to. Bends of a half step, whole step, major and minor thirds, and even larger intervals are possible. We will work with whole and half step bends for now. The following exercise practices whole step bends using the third and first fingers on the second string:

**Fig. 3**

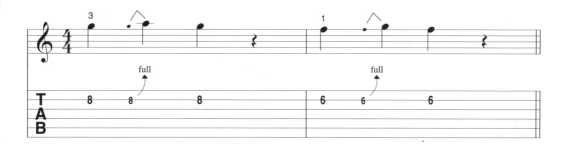

Practice this maneuver on the first, second, and third strings. The speed of the bend may also be varied. Try the exercise above bending upwards slowly, then quicker. Notice the effect? Now let's try some half-step bends on different strings:

**Fig. 4**

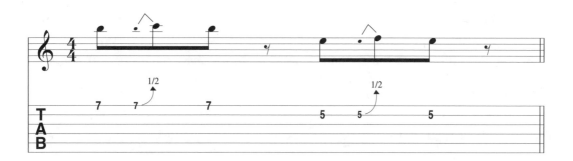

Make a mental note of how much energy it takes to produce the half-step bend as opposed to the whole-step bend. Let's look at a different bending technique, the *reverse bend*. The reverse bend (or pre-bend) begins with the note already bent up. The note is struck, then the bend is released down to the unbent note. Note how these are notated in the following figures.

**Fig. 5**

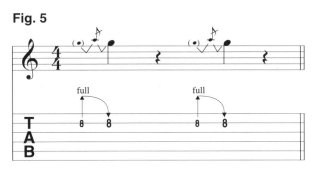

**Fig. 6**

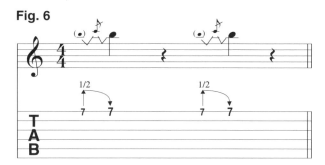

Notice the effect of the reverse bend?

Practice all of these figures on the first, second, and third strings. Of course notes on the fourth, fifth, and sixth strings may be bent, but it is easier to begin with the high strings. Sometimes, bends on the fourth, fifth, and sixth strings are pushed away from the supporting thumb, towards the floor. A lot of bends will be accompanied by vibrato (a rapid fluctuation of the volume or pitch of a note). This will be discussed separately.

## EXERCISE 2

Spend some time with your basic third and first finger bends before you work on this exercise. You should be able to bend and/or reverse bend in tune with both whole steps and half steps. This is often a hallmark of a strong guitarist—to be able to bend in tune, accurately every time! Exercise 2 uses the C major scale along the high E string as a departure point for bending notes. Use only your third finger for this exercise and practice it on all strings.

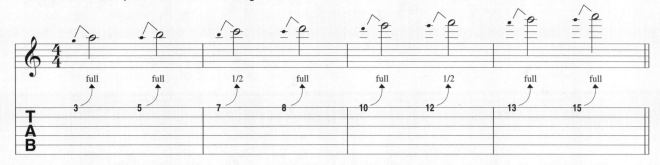

# Using Bends to Improvise in the Major Tonality

The question that usually comes up at this point is: which notes to bend? The simple answer is that you can bend up to any note in the major tonality. Let's narrow it down to some specific choices. In major tonality begin with bending the second degree (up to the third scale degree) and the fifth (up to the sixth scale degree). Play the following phrase over a G major chord:

**Fig. 7**

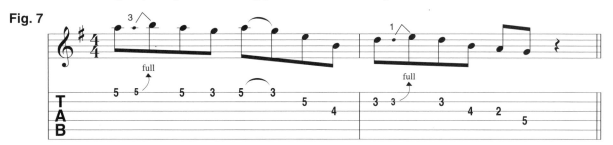

Can you hear it? Over the play-a-long progression (track 5), play phrases bending these pitches up a whole step.

Now try bending the third degree up a half step (to the fourth scale degree), and the seventh degree up a half step (to the tonic). Play the following figure which demonstrates this:

**Fig. 8**

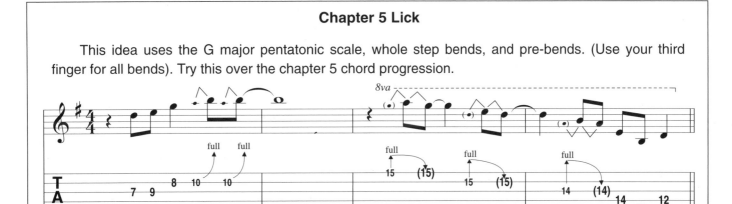

Can you hear it? Improvise over the play-a-long progression combining whole-step bends (of the second and fifth scale degrees) and half-step bends (of the third and seventh scale degrees). Try some reverse bends as well. Using the first and third fingers for bending may force you into changing the scale pattern fingerings a bit. This is fine. Try to remain flexible in your approach to fingerings. When you're comfortable with first and third finger bending, begin training the second and fourth fingers.

## Chapter 5 Lick

This idea uses the G major pentatonic scale, whole step bends, and pre-bends. (Use your third finger for all bends). Try this over the chapter 5 chord progression.

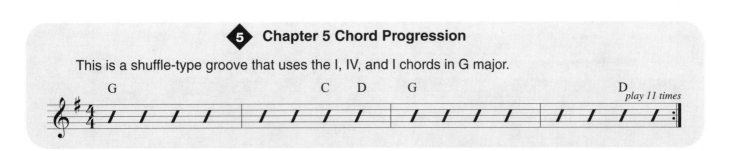

## 5 ▶ Chapter 5 Chord Progression

This is a shuffle-type groove that uses the I, IV, and I chords in G major.

| G | | | | C | D | G | | | D *play 11 times* |

## Chapter Five — REVIEW

1. Begin adding remaining patterns of the major pentatonic scale, keeping in line with long- and short-term goals.

2. Understand and be able to use technique pointers for bending.

3. Be able to perform whole- and half-step bends and whole- and half-step reverse bends.

4. Be able to improvise over major tonality chord progressions using bends of the suggested major tonality pitches.

# The Minor Scale

**6**

## Objectives

- To learn the construction of the minor scale.

- To learn two patterns of the minor scale.

- To apply sequences to the minor scale.

- To learn I, IV, and V chord progressions in the minor tonality.

- To improvise over minor tonality chord progressions.

### EXERCISE 1: Technique Exercise

This exercise is great for helping you develop the skills used in intervallic movements (string skipping). Accurate synchronization between your left and right hands is what's called for in this new variation of earlier finger combination exercises. Be sure not to play this faster than you can execute it (cleanly!).

(cont. up the fretboard)

## Construction of the Minor Scale

This scale is also called the natural minor scale and the Aeolian mode (scale). There are many types of minor scales. However, the natural minor is the basis of most minor harmony so we will begin our study of minor tonality with it.

The minor scale has half steps between the second and third degrees and the fifth and sixth degrees. From a C tonic, this yields the following notes:

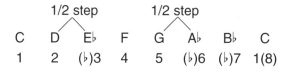

|     | 1/2 step |     |     | 1/2 step |     |     |       |
|-----|----------|-----|-----|----------|-----|-----|-------|
| C   | D        | E♭  | F   | G        | A♭  | B♭  | C     |
| 1   | 2        | (♭)3| 4   | 5        | (♭)6| (♭)7| 1(8)  |

It is important to note the two ways to view this scale. There is, obviously a relationship between C minor and E♭ major. These two scales share the same key signature, and they are the *relative major and minor* of each other. It is also important to be able to view the differences between *parallel keys*— that is, C major and C minor. An ability to see and hear major and minor keys in this way is crucial to good improvising.

# Patterns of the Natural Minor Scale

We will begin by learning patterns 2 and 4 for the natural minor scale. (Note that any scale whose tonics are located on the sixth, fourth, and first strings is named a pattern 4 scale. This idea will be used for all the other patterns as well.)

**Fig. 1**

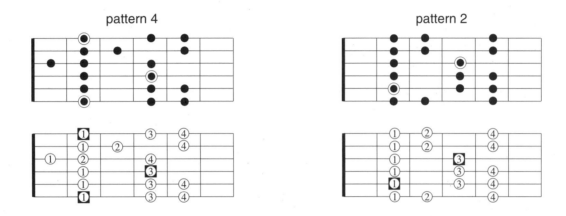

Practice these ascending and descending in all keys. Remember to start and end on the tonic so the minor tonality sound is "heard." Begin by using alternate picking. After you are comfortable with that, insert hammer-ons and pull-offs in different places.

## EXERCISE 2

Fill in the missing notes for the C natural minor-based ideas. You can use any note in the scale, any rhythm, hammer-ons, pull-offs, and bends.

# Sequencing the Natural Minor Scale

As with the major scale, sequences are one way to learn the patterns better and furnish ideas to help construct solos. Expand each of the following to the full range of the minor scale patterns. Again, alternate pick first, then use hammer-ons and pull-offs:

**Fig. 2: natural minor scale sequences**

# Chord Progressions in the Minor Tonality

Just like major tonality, we will begin the study of minor tonality harmony and chord progressions with I, IV, and V chords of the minor scale. When chords are built on these steps of the minor scale, the resulting triads are all minor. Listen to the suggested play-a-long progression in the key of C# minor (track 6 on the CD). Try to get a sense of the I, IV, and V chord sound in minor. One of the most basic aspects of music is the "happy, up" sound of major contrasting with the "sad, down" quality of minor. It is very important to be able to improvise in each of these tonalities, and combine them. The chapter 6 chord progression will be using the I, IV, and V chords of the minor scale. In later chapters, all the chords of the minor (and major) tonality will be utilized in these progressions.

# Improvising over Minor Tonality Chord Progressions

The play-a-long progression for this chapter is in C# minor.

The following figure demonstrates the use of the minor scale over this chord progression. Learn to play it slowly with the notated hammer-ons, pull-offs, and bends. Play it with a clean tone, then a distorted one. Remember to utilize all the technique pointers for playing with a distorted tone and bending.

**Fig. 3**

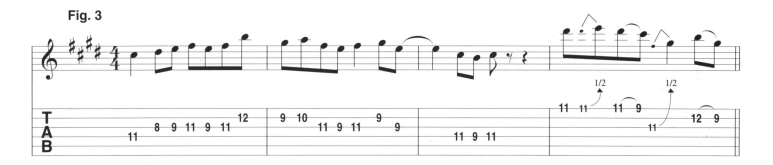

Begin to play with these techniques (hammer-ons, pull-offs, bending, distorted tone) all the time. Start to make every attempt at improvising as musical as possible.

---

### Chapter 6 Lick

Try this idea over the chapter 6 chord progression.

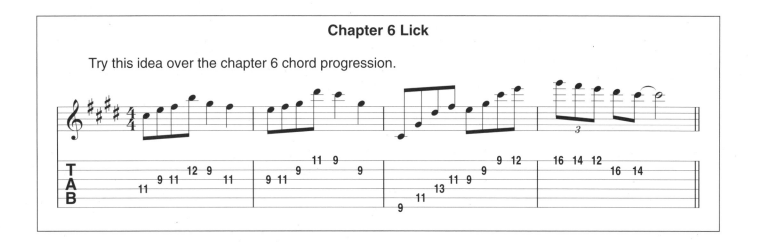

---

### 6 Chapter 6 Chord Progression

This is a I-IV-V progression in C# minor.

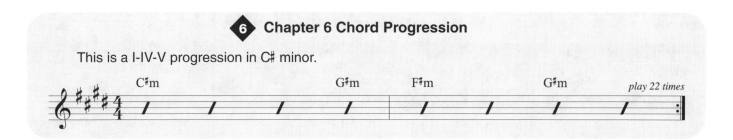

---

| Chapter Six | **REVIEW** |
| --- | --- |

1. Be able to construct a minor scale from any tonic.

2. Be able to play two patterns of the minor scale in any key.

3. Be able to play sequences ascending and descending through the entire range of minor scale patterns 2 and 4.

4. Be able to improvise over chord progressions that use I, IV, and V chords of the minor tonality, mixing alternate picking, hammer-ons, pull-offs, and distorted tone.

# Minor Scale Arpeggios

**7**

## Objectives

- To present the remaining patterns of the minor scale.
- To present shapes to arpeggiate the I, IV, and V chord triads of the minor scale in two patterns.
- To combine arpeggios and scale movement in the minor tonality.
- To discuss the different techniques of vibrato and incorporate them into your improvisation.
- To combine arpeggios, minor scales, and vibrato over minor tonality chord progressions.

### Exercise 1: Stretching Exercise

Hold your right hand palm up (toward the ceiling), grab the fingers with your left hand and gently stretch your fingers downwards toward the floor. Do this slowly, and breathe deeply. Change hands and stretch the left side.

## Patterns of the Natural Minor Scale

Here are the remaining patterns of the natural minor scale. Again, keep the long and short term goals in mind. Move on to these patterns only after patterns 2 and 4 are available for immediate recall and use in any key.

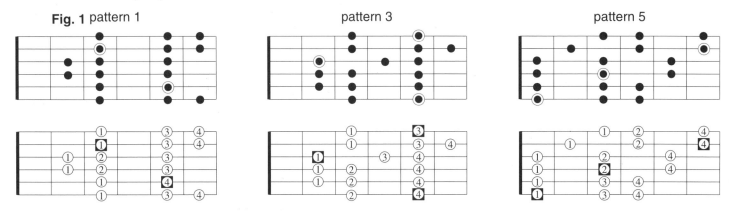

**Fig. 1** pattern 1          pattern 3          pattern 5

When ready, be able to play these on any tonic, ascending and descending using alternate picking, then using hammer-ons and pull-offs.

## Arpeggio Shapes for the I, IV, and V Chords of the Minor Tonality

As was stated in the previous chapter, the I, IV, and V chords of the minor scale are all minor triads. The following diagrams show the triad arpeggio shapes for these chords in the lower octave of pattern 4:

**Fig. 2 – pattern 4 lower octave**

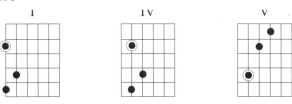

I          I V          V

Be able to play each of these ascending and descending. The triads in the upper octave are as follows:

**Fig. 3 – pattern 4 upper octave**

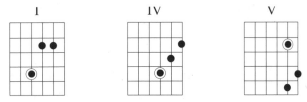

Now look at these arpeggios in the lower octave of pattern 2:

**Fig. 4 – pattern 2 lower octave**

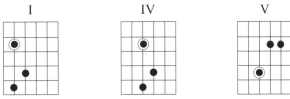

Practice these ascending and descending in all keys using alternate picking, then applying hammer-ons and pull-offs.

# Combining Minor Scales and Arpeggios

The following figure combines scale and arpeggio movement over a minor tonality chord progression in the key of A minor:

Fig. 5

**EXERCISE 2**

Now, write one of these studies on your own. Try to do it in a different pattern of the minor scale. Use hammer-ons, pull-offs, bends, and arpeggios from the I, IV, and V chords.

# Techniques of Vibrato

Vibrato is one of the most expressive devices a musician has. It is one of the factors contributing to a player's "signature" sound; many players can be identified by their vibrato only! What is vibrato? Vibrato is a fluctuation of a note's pitch or volume. Most guitarists use a fluctuation of pitch to produce this effect, actually using a slight bend. Here a few ways to achieve it:

**Method #1:**

With the tip of any fretting finger "draw" a circle over a fretted pitch. This moves the string, producing a slight bend.

**Method #2:**

While fretting a note, move the wrist towards, then away from the fingerboard (thereby moving the finger, which bends the string slightly).

The first two methods actually change the pitch of the fretted note slightly. *The speed of the vibrato can also be altered. Try a fast and slow vibrato by speeding up or slowing down the methods above.*

**Method #3:**

This approach is more of a change in volume. While fretting a note, press into the notes, and rock your finger lengthwise along the string, within that fret. It should be a "pulsing" effect.

# Single String/Improv Foundations

As you can see, there are many methods of producing vibrato, and each sounds slightly different. Experiment with each of the methods above, producing slow, and faster vibratos. Vibratos are notated with a wavy line above the designated note:

**Fig. 6**

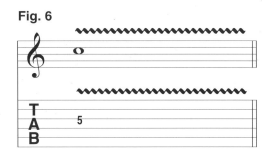

Play the following phrases using any of the methods described above to vibrato the selected notes:

**Fig. 7: phrases using vibrato**

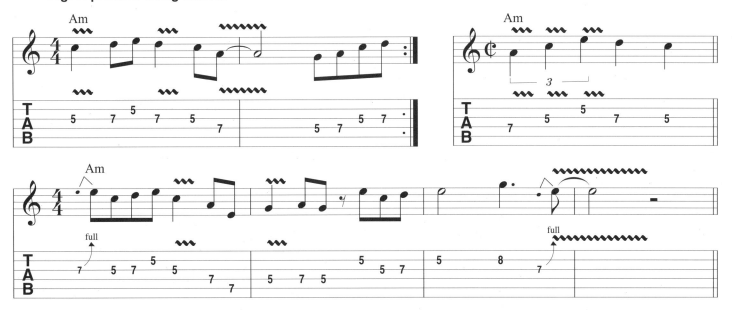

This technique should make your phrases more musical and expressive to the listener.

## Chapter 7 Lick

This is a fast Rock-style lick with some neoclassical ideas, bends, and vibrato. Play it over the chapter 7 chord progression.

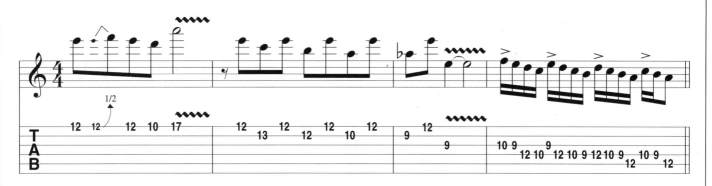

## 7 Chapter 7 Chord Progression

This is a fast straight eighth note I–IV–V groove in Am.

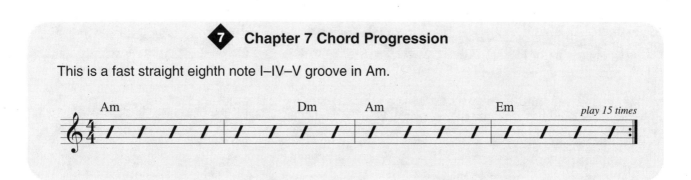

| Chapter Seven | REVIEW |
| --- | --- |

1. Understand long and short term goals for learning all patterns of the natural minor scale.

2. Be able to arpeggiate the I, IV, and V chord triads in two patterns, in any minor key.

3. Be able to mix arpeggio, and scale movement over minor tonality chord progressions on the play-along CD.

4. Be able to produce vibrato with each of the three methods described above.

5. Be able to use vibrato while improvising over minor (and major) tonality chord progressions.

# The Minor Pentatonic Scale

**8**

## Objectives

- To learn the construction of the minor pentatonic scale.
- To learn two patterns of the minor pentatonic scale.
- To sequence the minor Pentatonic scale.
- To use slides.
- To combine the minor and the minor pentatonic scale over minor tonality chord progressions.

### EXERCISE 1 – Technique Exercise

This exercise is another variation of our original 1-2-3-4 finger combination exercise. This time you will be stretching an extra fret (a whole step!) between your third and fourth fingers as you ascend and descend.

*(cont. up fretboard)*

## The Construction of the Minor Pentatonic Scale

The minor pentatonic scale is derived from the minor scale. Leaving out the second and sixth degrees of the minor scale gives us the notes of the minor pentatonic scale. From a tonic of E, this yields the following notes:

| E | G | A | B | D | E |
|---|---|---|---|---|---|
| 1 | (♭)3 | 4 | 5 | (♭)7 | 1(8) |

The minor pentatonic scale is a widely used sound in rock, blues, and other styles. It can be used wherever the minor scale is used, if the improviser desires that "sound."

## Patterns of the Minor Pentatonic Scale

As was stated above, the notes (and patterns) for the minor pentatonic scale are derived from the minor scale, and the fingering patterns reflect this. These patterns look like the major pentatonic scales beginning on the sixth degree. This can be an easier way to view these patterns, but it can also be confusing. We recommend learning these patterns, and practicing them from the tonic, thereby imprinting the sound of these scales in the player's ears. Here are Patterns 2 and 4 of the minor pentatonic scale:

**Fig. 1**

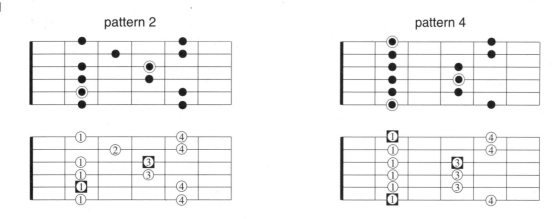

Be able to play these patterns from any tonic, ascending and descending, with alternate picking, then using hammer-ons and pull-offs.

# Sequencing the Minor Pentatonic Scale

Sequencing helps get the scale sound in our ears and gives us ideas to use in our solos. However, sequences should not be looked at as the "be all and end all" of ways to make these scales turn into music. Phrases, ways to develop solos, licks, and solos from artists are invaluable tools as well. In time, all of these areas should be studied and assimilated. For now, learn the following sequences, applying them to the full range of notes in the patterns given. Be able to play these in any minor key.

**Fig. 2: minor pentatonic sequences**

# Using Slides

*Sliding* is a very natural act on the guitar. It can mean sliding up to or down to a note from one note in particular, or using the same finger to go between different notes on the same string. It is notated with a short diagonal line, pointed in the direction of the intended slide. Play the following notes by sliding from below (or above):

**Fig. 3**

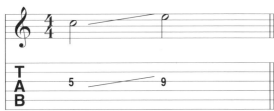

**Fig. 4**

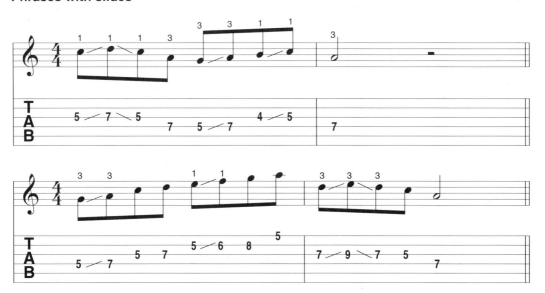

When executing a slide between two specific notes this action can be performed in two different ways. Look at the figure on the left:

One way to perform this is to play the first note, stop its sounding, then move to the second note. The other way is to allow the note to continue ringing while moving the same finger along the string to the second note, thus hearing all the pitches in between (known as a *glissando*). Practice the example using both techniques. The first technique should sound like you are in the same postition, whereas the second should really sound like you are going somewhere. It is a very expressive sound (the second approach). However, using this technique does move the player up and down the fingerboard and if one does not know the scale patterns, an unknown area of the neck could cause trouble. Slides should be practiced staying within the fingering patterns you know for now. This may take some adjustments of the fingerings in these patterns, so remain flexible in your approach. Play the following phrases. Pay close attention to the fingerings:

**Fig. 5 – Phrases with slides**

**EXERCISE 2: Sliding between Scale Degrees 4 and 5**

Play the following minor pentatonic scale patterns using the suggested slides. Notice how effective the technique of sliding can be for linking together shapes, patterns, licks, and covering a wide range of position movements on the fretboard.

# Combining the Minor, and Minor Pentatonic Scales over a Minor Tonality Chord

**8** **Chapter 8 Chord Progression**

The following chord progression is in the key of B minor and uses a straight-eighth feel in 4/4.

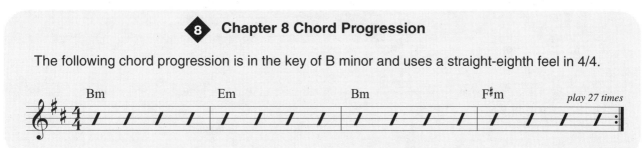

All of the following figures may be played over the chapter 8 chord progression. Let's begin with a familiar figure by ascending the minor scale and descending the minor pentatonic scale:

**Fig. 6**

Now, let's reverse it:

**Fig. 7**

The following four-measure study combines these two scales:

**Fig. 8**

Once you can perform these examples, play them over and over, inserting the different performance possibilities such as distorted or clean tone, hammer-ons, pull-offs, slides, bends, and vibrato. Notice how even the simplest of phrases will take on more musical meaning and emotion with the addition of these techniques.

## Chapter 8 Lick

Try this idea over the chapter 8 chord progression; it uses whole step bends, a slide and hammer-on/pull-off technique and is based around B minor pentatonic pattern 4. When you are able, try transposing this lick into different keys. Be sure to play this idea with both clean and distorted tones, then decide which one sounds best.

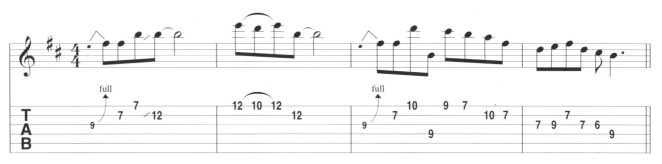

| **Chapter Eight** | **REVIEW** |
|---|---|

1. Be able to construct the minor pentatonic scale from any tonic.

2. Be able to play two patterns of the minor pentatonic scale ascending and descending from any tonic.

3. Be able to apply the given sequences ascending and descending through the entire range of two patterns of the minor pentatonic scale.

4. Be able to use slides.

5. Be able to combine the minor and minor pentatonic scales over a minor tonality chord progression, applying all performance techniques (clean and distorted tone, hammer-ons and pull-offs, bends, and vibrato).

# Minor Pentatonic Phrases

## Objectives

- To present the remaining patterns of the minor pentatonic scale.

- To learn minor pentatonic scale phrases.

- To apply all performance techniques (hammer-ons, pull-offs, slides, vibrato, bending, clean, and distorted tone) to a given solo.

### EXERCISE 1: Technique Exercise

This chapter's technique exercise is another finger combination variation that uses a stretch between fingers of the fretting hand. The stretch is a whole step that occurs between fingers 1 and 2. It is exactly the same pattern ascending and descending.

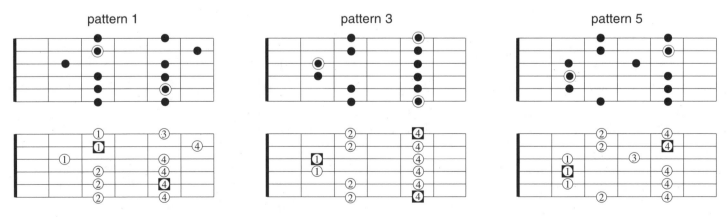

## Remaining Minor Pentatonic Scale Patterns

Here are patterns 1, 3, and 5 of the minor pentatonic scale. Learn these, applying all sequences and picking possibilities when ready.

pattern 1          pattern 3          pattern 5

# Minor Pentatonic Scale Phrases

The following phrases are of various lengths and are from the minor pentatonic scale. Play them over progressions in the given keys:

**Fig. 2**

It is very important to move these phrases around. In other words, play them in different positions, patterns, and keys. Try to change them a little bit to your own taste by adding or taking notes away. This will help you to recall and play them more quickly.

# Applying Performance Techniques to a Given Solo

The next figure is a solo based on the chapter 9 chord progression (track 9 on the play-a-long CD). The TAB has been left blank and there are no performance tips given. This is so you can experiment with interpreting the solo in your own way. The best idea is to first choose a pattern to play the example in and then randomly apply slides, hammer-ons, pull-offs, and vibrato using either a clean or distorted tone. Take some time and really decide where you like to hear each of the slides or hammer-ons and pull-offs. Which notes sound best with vibrato? Which vibrato technique will you use? Which notes do you wish to hear using bending? When you have fully decided where to use all or some of these techniques, notate them on the staff and TAB. Ultimately, the player should be applying these techniques from the inception of the melodic phrase being performed.

**Fig. 3**

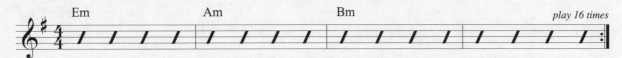

### Chapter 9 Chord Progression

This is a 4/4 straight eighth rock groove with the I, IV, and V chords in E minor.

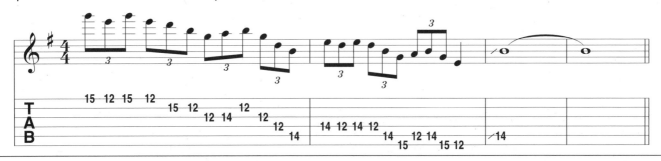

### Chapter 9 Lick

Try this idea over the chapter 9 chord progression. This lick is played entirely in E minor pentatonic pattern 4. Add hammer-ons and pull-offs, if desired.

---

**Chapter Nine**                    **REVIEW**

1. When ready, learn more minor pentatonic scale patterns and apply sequences to them.

2. Be able to play the given minor pentatonic scale phrases in other patterns, positions, and keys.

3. Be able to play the given solo using all performance techniques and notate them on the given staves.

# Three Note-Per-String
# 10 Major Scales

## Objectives

- To learn to play the major scales in three note-per-string configuration.
- To learn exercises and phrases in three note-per-string format.
- To learn "one string" exercises.
- Using three note-per-string scale patterns over major tonality chord progressions.

### EXERCISE 1: Creativity Exercise

This is the "Chinese menu" approach. It helps you forge new sounds and combinations that might not normally happen in your playing habits. Choose a rhythm (for example: triplets), choose a scale and key (for example: D major pentatonic) and then choose a technique (for example: hammer-ons). Then play a solo (or "noodle" around) with these three parameters. Try out three different possibilities each day.

## Three Note-per-String Major Scales

The five major scale patterns that have been used up to this point are only one way to play this scale. There is another system based on three notes per string which yields seven patterns. The previous major scale pattern 5 is an example of this.

**Fig. 1: major scale fingering pattern 5, three note-per-string pattern 1**

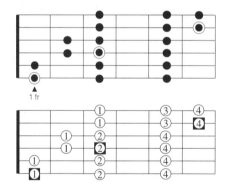

By moving up the neck (in the key of F major), starting on the second pitch of the scale, then the third, and so on, the following shapes are derived:

**Fig. 2**

three note-per-string pattern 2    three note-per-string pattern 3    three note-per-string pattern 4

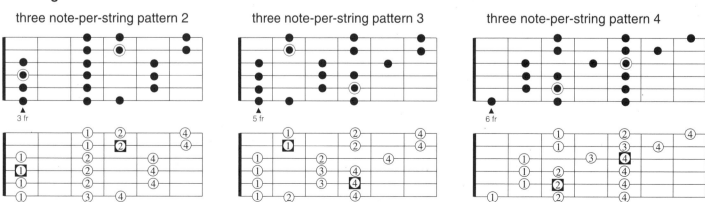

three note-per-string pattern 5     three note-per-string pattern 6     three note-per-string pattern 7

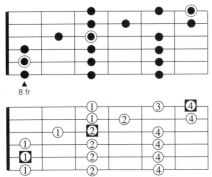
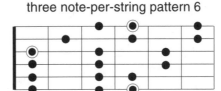
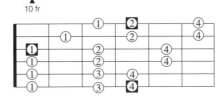
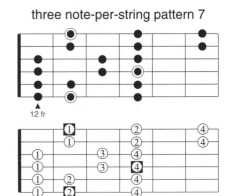

What is the advantage of these, you may ask? Many players find this an easier and speedier way to play the scales. They require a bit of a stretch, and are not quite as easy to compare to the chord shapes, but these shapes do have some physical advantages. In terms of picking, some players find it difficult to mix two and three note-per-string shapes, and the three-note approach seems easier to play fast. Others consider this approach a more "speed metal" or specific stylistic device.

### EXERCISE 2: Four Note-per-String Major Scale

For an even longer version of a major scale shape, try this four note-per-string shape that covers the entire fretboard by stretching and sliding an F major scale from the first fret to the seventeenth fret. There are actually many ways to play and connect your scale patterns. You may want to explore some of the possibilities of this on your own. Use the "one string" exercises (in the next section) combined with the new three note-per-string scale patterns and/or the traditional five scale patterns to create your own hybrid shapes.

# Exercises and Phrases in the Three Note-per-String Patterns

These patterns lend themselves to different kinds of phrases and exercises. Play these two examples using alternate picking:

**Fig. 3**

Here's how these two figures may be combined to create an exercise through the entire pattern, ascending and descending:

### EXERCISE 3

Note the motions of the pick. When ascending, the pick crosses over "outside" the strings, descending it crosses "inside" the strings. These two motions feel different, and it is helpful for the student to be aware of this and to practice both.

Apply this exercise to the three note-per-string pattern 5 (whose tonic is on the fifth, third, and first strings). Play the following phrases based on these patterns:

**Fig. 4**

## "One String" Exercises

All of our playing so far has revolved around remaining in basically one position on the neck. These new patterns force the student to shift and stretch the positions. "One string" exercises are sequences which ascend and descend on a single string. The following sequence, in the key of C, is played on the second string only. Note the fingerings:

### EXERCISE 4

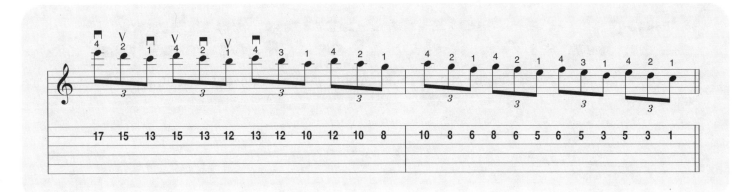

By applying this exercise to other strings (ultimately all of them) in the same key, a picture of the entire neck starts to emerge. This exercise is on the fourth string in the key of C:

**EXERCISE 5**

Play the following one string exercises. Begin with the second string, and play them ascending and descending a full octave, as in the previous exercise. Note the fingerings:

**EXERCISE 6**                                          **EXERCISE 7**

Changing position and connecting up all the patterns on the neck will be gone into in greater depth in upcoming chapters. The three note patterns, with their inherent stretches, lend themselves easily to these one string exercises.

# Using Three Note-per-String Patterns over Major Tonality Chord Progressions

The following study uses three note-per-string patterns in D major, over track #10 (the chapter 10 chord progression) from the play-a-long CD:

**Fig. 5**

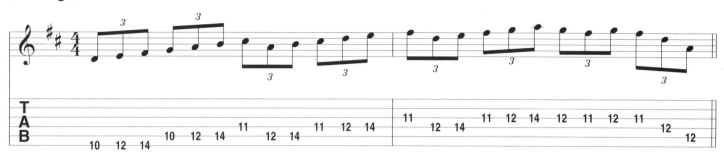

**10** **Chapter 10 Chord Progression**

This is a fast shuffle in D major.

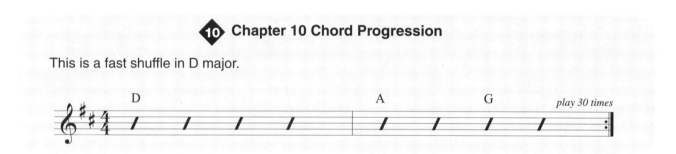

Notice how the pattern in figure 5 lends itself to a triplet feel. Now improvise over track #10 using sixteenth notes. Use hammer-ons and pull-offs if the tempo is too fast to alternate pick. Play the following study:

**Fig. 6**

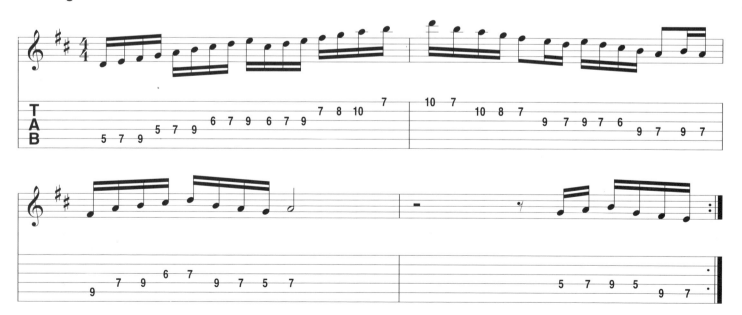

You should now be able to improvise using two patterns of the three note-per-string patterns. When ready, use the "one string" exercises to move up and down the neck to other patterns.

## Chapter 10 Lick

Use this lick over the chapter 10 chord progression. Pay attention to the fingerings; think of small triadic chord shapes. It may take some time to get this one up to the tempo on the CD!

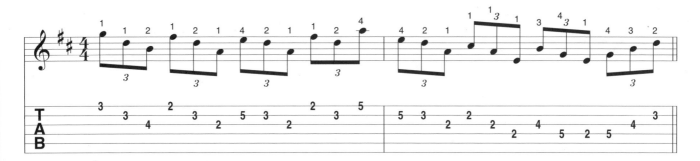

---

| Chapter Ten | REVIEW |
| --- | --- |

1. Be able to play two patterns of the three note-per-string major scales ascending and descending.

2. Be able to play the given exercises and phrases in two of the three note-per-string patterns.

3. Be able to play the "one string" exercises given.

4. Be able to improvise over major tonality chord progressions with these new patterns.

# 11 Economy Picking and Three Note-Per String Minor Scales

## Objectives

- To present three note-per-string patterns for the minor scale.
- To learn and use economy picking.
- To apply staccato and legato techniques.
- To apply all devices over a minor tonality chord progression.

### EXERCISE 1: Technique Exercise

This chapter's exercise is yet another variation of our 1-2-3-4 finger combination exercise. In eighth notes: jump to random positions on the fretboard. Try to make "daredevil" leaps, as you stay "in time" with the metronome. Try this exercise with triplet and sixteenth note rhythms, too. For example:

## Three Note-per-String Minor Scales

We will continue with three note-per-string scale patterns; this time in the natural minor scale. Note the locations of the tonics in all of the following patterns (in the key of F minor).

Concentrate on learning patterns 1 and 5. Apply all the exercises from the previous chapter (three note-per-string patterns in major scale) to these minor scale patterns.

**Fig. 1**                    three note-per-string pattern 1

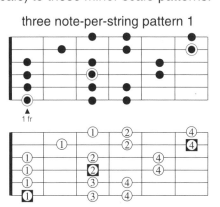

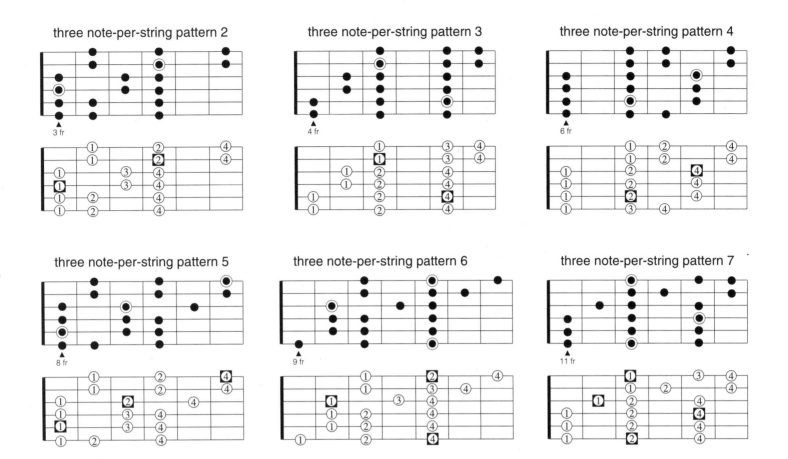

three note-per-string pattern 2

three note-per-string pattern 3

three note-per-string pattern 4

three note-per-string pattern 5

three note-per-string pattern 6

three note-per-string pattern 7

# Economy Picking

*Economy picking* is another method for training the picking hand. It involves playing consecutive up or downstrokes when crossing strings. This saves motion in the picking hand. Play the following figure:

**Fig. 2**

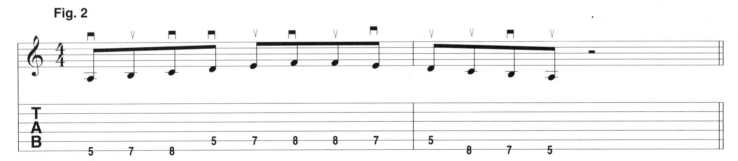

Notice when crossing from the sixth to the fifth strings, two downstrokes were used. When descending and crossing from the fifth to the sixth string, two upstrokes were used. This type of picking should be practiced slowly at first, as consecutive downstrokes tend to speed up a little bit (you're going with gravity!), and consecutive upstrokes tend to drag a little bit (you're going against gravity!). This next exercise ascends and descends the minor scale using economy picking.

**Fig. 3**

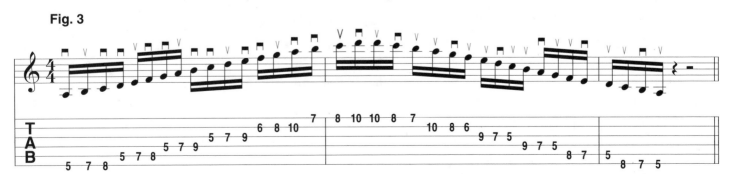

These next examples mix up the notes of the minor scale. Note the pick directions:

**Fig. 4**

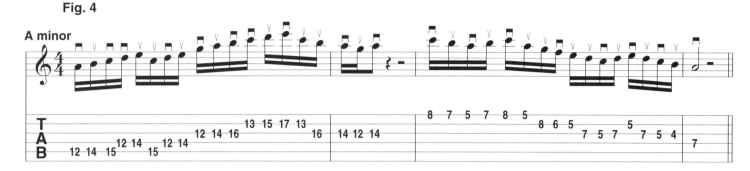

This is another way of producing notes on the guitar, and it is not meant to replace any previous methods. The idea is to add this technique to your practicing, and eventually your playing. How should you pick a certain phrase? There really is no one answer. All methods should be experimented with, the ultimate choice resting on how the player wishes to make it sound!

# Staccato and Legato

*Staccato* and *legato* are two more items to add to our list of "performance techniques" (bends, vibrato, etc...). These are subtle things, yet some players would say they are the most important, as they add emotion and expressiveness to your music.

Staccato is a technique in which the note is played shorter than notated. It is deadened by either lifting the fretting finger or muting with the palm. This gives a slight accent effect as well. The notes should sound "clipped." Play the following exercise in a staccato fashion. Use alternate picking, as this seems to give better control for this particular technique.

**EXERCISE 2: Staccato Exercise**

Legato is the opposite of staccato in that the notes are left to ring out as long as possible. The notes are played smoothly, with no separation between them. On the guitar this is usually achieved by leaving the fingers down as long as possible, and using hammer-ons and pull-offs to smooth the initial attack of the note. Three note-per-string patterns lend themselves to legato style playing very easily, especially with a smooth distorted tone. Play the following exercise with a distorted tone, and get a "smooth" sound from note to note using hammer-ons and pull-offs:

**EXERCISE 3: Legato Exercise**

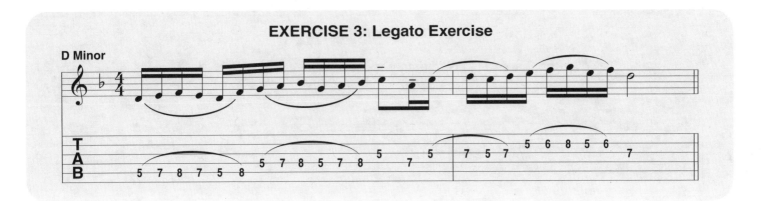

Go through all of your favorite licks in this book (or your own) and practice adding staccato and legato on the spot. Notice how each of the licks takes on a whole new character with the addition of these techniques.

# Using Three Note-per-String Patterns and Staccato and Legato over Minor Tonality Chord Progressions

Learn the following example based on track 7 (the chapter 11 chord progression) from the CD. After you are able to play it, experiment with using staccato and legato in different places. Notice that where you place these devices alters the effect of the line each time. Improvise on your own. Try mixing three note-per-string patterns with previously learned patterns. Use all performance techniques. Express yourself!

**Fig. 5**

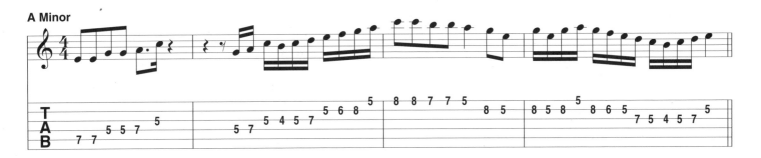

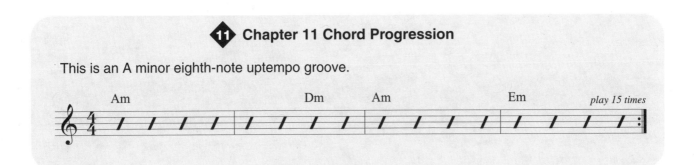

**🔷11 Chapter 11 Chord Progression**

This is an A minor eighth-note uptempo groove.

## Chapter 11 Lick

Use this lick over the Chapter 11 chord progression

| | Chapter Eleven | **REVIEW** |
| --- | --- | --- |

1. Be able to play two three note-per-string minor scale patterns (patterns 1 and 5).

2. Be able to demonstrate and use economy picking.

3. Be able to improvise over the suggested play-a-long progression in three note-per-string minor scale patterns using staccato and legato techniques.

# Major Arpeggios

## Objectives

- To learn one and two octave major arpeggios based on the five patterns.

- To learn exercises and phrases based on the major arpeggios.

- To combine major arpeggios and major scales over major tonality chord progressions.

### EXERCISE 1: Stretching Exercise

This is a bit more complex stretch, but it is very effective for the wrist and forearm if done slowly. Hold your right arm out directly in front of your body (as if to shake hands with someone). Rotate your hand so that the thumb points downwards towards the floor. Grab the right hand with the left hand, and slowly draw it in towards your body, forming a "Z" shape in the arm. As you get closer to your body with the hands, you may want to increase the stretch by pointing the fingers of the right hand upwards (to the ceiling). Hold this position of maximum comfortable stretch for a moment, then switch to the left side and repeat the exercise. This can be a very powerful stretch, so take it slowly and easily at first!

## Major Arpeggios

Earlier in this course we looked at triad arpeggios. *Major arpeggios* are expanded triads in that they cover the entire range of a fingering pattern with the root, third, and fifth. The following shapes are based on the original five patterns (not the three note-per-string patterns). They cover the entire range of each pattern. Some of these shapes are a full two octaves while others are a little larger than an octave. Play these shapes using alternate picking starting on the root. Other methods of picking these shapes will be addressed shortly.

**Fig. 1**

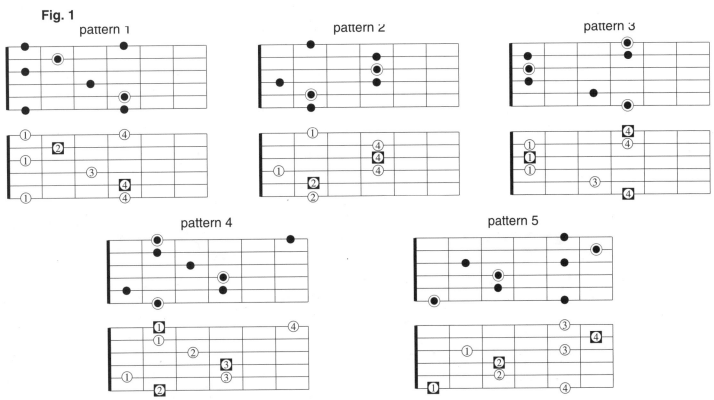

# Sequences and Phrases Based on the Major Arpeggios

Here are some sequences to apply to the full range of the major arpeggio shapes. Use alternate picking. These figures will be a challenge for the picking hand as there are a lot of string skips involved!:

**Fig. 2: major arpeggio sequences**

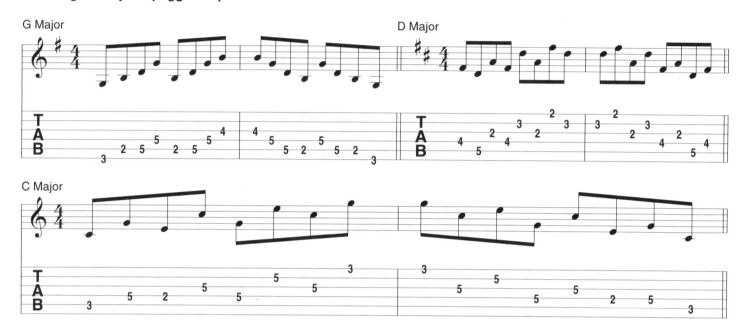

These next examples are phrases that combine some scalar motion with the arpeggio shapes. Try inserting some hammer-ons and pull-offs, as well as all the other performance techniques, once you have learned these phrases.

**Fig. 3: major arpeggio/scale phrases**

# Combining Major Scales and Major Arpeggios over Major Tonality Chord Progressions

This next figure is based on track 5 (the chapter 12 chord progression) from the play-a-long CD. As in previous examples, learn it using alternate picking, then apply all performance techniques and picking possibilities:

**Fig. 4**

### ⬥12 Chapter 12 Chord Progression

Chord progression 1 is a shuffle in G major.

### Chapter 12 Lick

Play this lick over the chapter 12 chord progression. It uses major arpeggios, diatonic sixth interval skips, and other notes from G major.

## EXERCISE 2

Write your own four-measure idea for the chapter 12 chord progression below using major arpeggios (mainly) and notes of the G major scale. Remember that you will use the notes that "outline" or spell out each chord; in other words, you will play a G major arpeggio over the G chord and then switch to a D major arpeggio over the D chord, etc. The main point is to try to link your note choices in a smooth way using notes and rhythms that sound good to your ears. Don't be too concerned about playing a lot of notes, or playing too "intellectually."

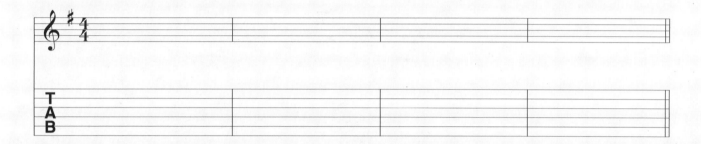

| **Chapter Twelve** | **REVIEW** |
| --- | --- |

1. Be able to play at least three patterns of the major arpeggio shapes presented.

2. Be able to apply the given sequences to three patterns of the major arpeggios.

3. Be able to play figure 4 and the chapter 12 lick over the chapter 12 chord progression (track 5 on the CD) using all performance techniques.

4. Be able to mix scalar arpeggiated movement over the suggested major tonality chord progressions.

# 13 Minor Arpeggios and Sweep Picking

## Objectives

- To learn one and two octave minor arpeggios based on the five patterns.

- To learn sequences and phrases based on the minor arpeggios.

- To learn sweep picking exercises and apply it to arpeggios.

- To combine minor arpeggios and minor scales over minor tonality chord progressions.

### EXERCISE 1: Technique Exercise

This exercise is another variation of the 1-2-3-4 finger combination exercise. You will be working to improve synchronization of the hands by making interval leaps. Also, pay attention to your tone as you do this exercise. Are there any muffled notes? Missed pick attacks? Be sure that you are able to hear each note clearly and cleanly!

(cont. up the fretboard)

## Minor Arpeggios

Let's continue to work with arpeggios, focusing on minor arpeggios. The following shapes are based on the original five patterns of the minor scale. They cover the entire range of each pattern. Some of these shapes are a full two octaves while others are a little larger than an octave:

**Fig. 1**

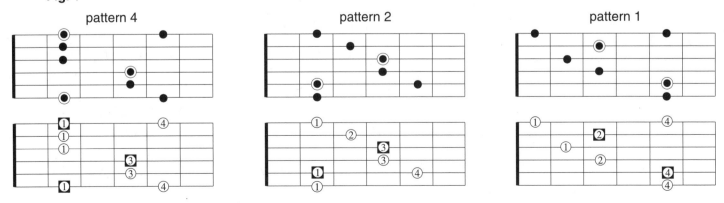

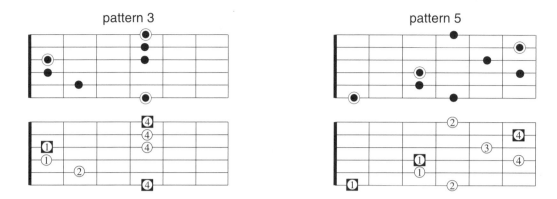

pattern 3  pattern 5

Play these shapes using alternate picking starting on the root.

# Sequences and Phrases Based on the Minor Arpeggio Shapes

Apply the following sequences to the full range of the arpeggios, ascending and descending. Use alternate picking. (These exercises will be a challenge for the picking hand as there are a lot of string skips involved!):

**Fig. 2: minor arpeggio sequences**

These next examples are phrases that combine some scalar motion with the arpeggio shapes:

**Fig. 3: major scale/arpeggio phrases**

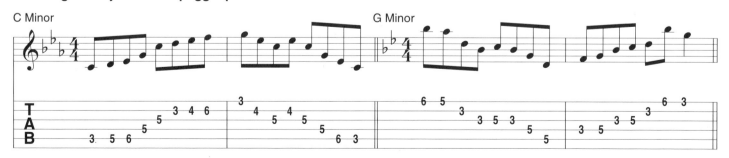

Try inserting some hammer-ons and pull-offs, as well as all the other performance techniques, once you have learned these phrases.

# Sweep Picking

*Sweep picking* is a term used to describe consecutive down or upstrokes on two or more adjacent strings. This method works well with arpeggio shapes as they tend to have only one note on a string. Sweep picking also has a smooth horn-like sound and can conserve right hand energy. As with economy picking, sweep picking is not meant to replace any former picking systems, it is another way to produce notes that should be at the players command. Let's begin with a look at the physical elements of this concept.

The following exercise uses the top three open strings. The three consecutive downstrokes should be performed as one movement. Make a special note of this for the upstrokes as the player will tend to make three separate motions. As the name implies, "sweep" or drag the pick through the strings, allowing it to rest on the next string before producing an attack:

**Fig. 4**

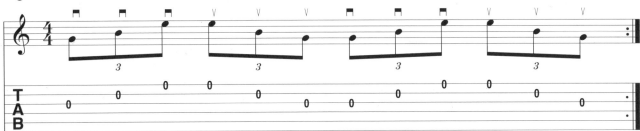

Try not to change the angle of the hand (and therefore the pick!) on the upstrokes as this will change the sound. Now try sweeping the top four strings:

**Fig. 5**

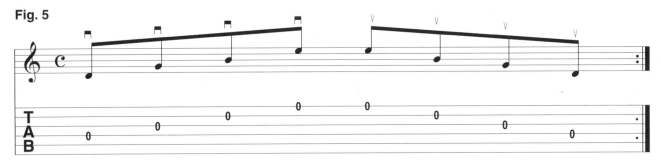

Let's add some notes to the three string sweep. When playing notes in this way, the finger must be lifted after the note is struck, otherwise all the notes of the sweep will run together. (When sweeping a barre, the finger must be rolled to stop previous notes from ringing.) Be careful of the timing so all notes are heard evenly:

**Fig. 6**

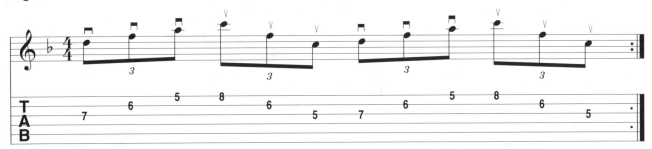

Now we'll add some notes which will be picked alternately, then sweep back down:

**Fig. 7**

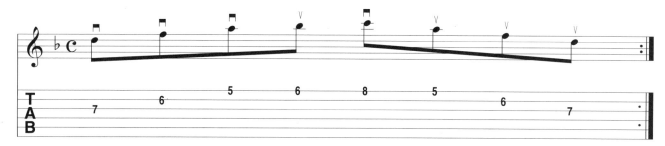

Let's add some notes to the four string sweep:

**Fig. 8**

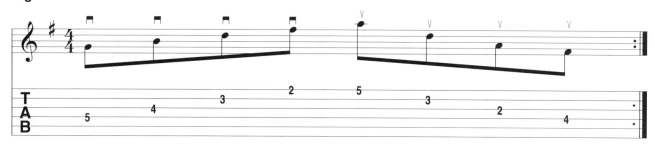

Entire arpeggios can be played using this approach:

**Fig. 9**

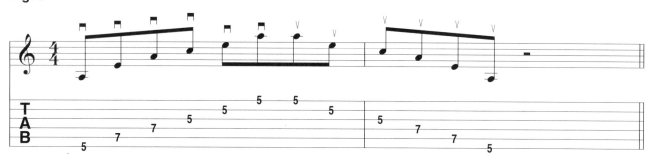

Notice that one note was left out of the previous arpeggio so that there was only one note per string. There are other ways in which that note may be added, and sweep picking still incorporated by using a hammer-on or by starting with an upstroke:

**Fig. 10**

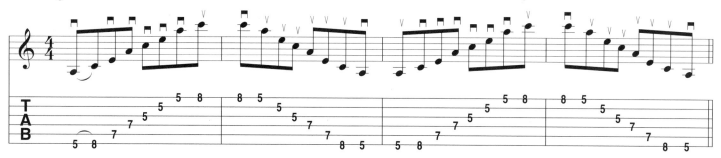

These exercises only scratch the surface of this topic. The player needs to get comfortable with the basic physical aspects of sweeping and after doing this, licks of this nature can be seen using many chord shapes.

Practice this technique very slowly, making sure all attacks sound even, The tendency is to rush the sweep, but you will lose the definition of each note if you do this! Practice slowly, and don't change the angle of your hand (pick) from downstroke to upstroke!

This short study uses the I, V, and IV arpeggios of G minor (measures 1-2) and G major (measures 3-4). There are lots of small sweeps in this, and be prepared to change positions!

**Fig. 11: practice etude**

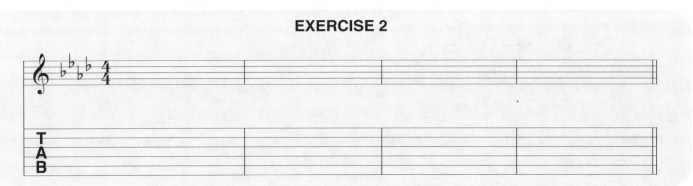

# Combining Minor Scales and Minor Arpeggios over Minor Tonality Chord Progressions

Using track 11 (the chapter 13 chord progression) on the play-a-long CD, write an example in the four measures provided. Use scale and arpeggio motion, and perform it using all devices. Keep on refining your note choice and use of performance techniques until you can play your own example with these techniques in different places every time.

**EXERCISE 2**

**13 Chapter 13 Chord Progression**

This chord progression is a fast F minor shuffle.

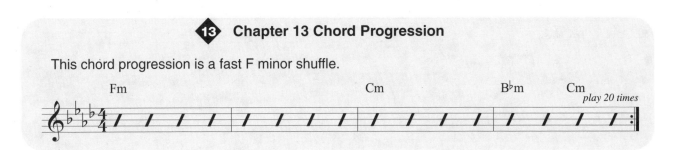

## Chapter 13 Lick

Play this idea over the chapter 13 chord progression. The tempo is fast! Use hammer-ons and/or sweep picking performance techniques. Measures 1 and 2 use a pentatonic sequence, 3 and 4 use minor arpeggios.

| Chapter Thirteen | REVIEW |
|---|---|

1. Be able to play at least three patterns of the minor arpeggio shapes presented.

2. Be able to apply the given sequences to three patterns of the minor arpeggios.

3. Be able to play basic sweep picking exercises and examples.

4. Be able to play the self composed example over track 11 (the chapter 13 chord progression) on the CD using all performance techniques.

5. Be able to mix scalar and arpeggiated movement over the suggested minor tonality chord progressions.

# Connecting All Patterns

## 14

## Objectives

- To begin studying the ways to change position on the fingerboard, connecting up all patterns using:
    1. Sliding
    2. Stretching
    3. Position Shifting.

---

**EXERCISE 1: Visualization Exercise**

Spend some time daily playing your guitar with your eyes closed. This can be done in a Single String (improvising, melodic playing) context, or you can also do this with chords. You may want to visualize a scale pattern, lick, or other melodic shape, and then try to play; eyes closed. Or, you may want to play freely over rhythm tracks, with a friend or alone, with your eyes closed. The focus is on making music, and on really listening to your playing. Your "musical instinct" will grow from doing this.

---

## Changing Positions on the Fingerboard

The next two chapters will deal with changing positions on the fingerboard. Guitarists seem especially guilty of remaining in one position. This limits the expressive range of one's playing. Moving up and down the fingerboard gives the player a wider range of colors to work with. On the guitar this takes some work. The first part of the work is having a good knowledge of the five fingering patterns. This may take some time, but as you get to see these patterns more clearly, shifting around the neck will be much easier. The second part is the physical act of changing position smoothly. There are three ways to change position on the fingerboard:

1. *Sliding:* This is the act of playing two consecutive notes with the same finger, moving up or down the fingerboard. (Don't confuse this with glissando!).

2. *Stretching:* This involves wider distances between the fingers of the fretting hand to cover more frets.

3. *Position Shifting:* This means moving the entire hand to a different position on the neck, with a different finger for the next note.

Let's look at each of these areas:

## Changing Positions Using Sliding

This is probably the easiest method for changing positions—by just using the same finger to move to a note higher (or lower) on the same string. Don't confuse this with a glissando, where all the notes in between the two notes you're sliding are heard. We want a clean slide, so release a little bit of pressure in between these two pitches. This next example uses a major scale to demonstrate connecting pattern 4 of G major to pattern 5 of the same scale:

**Fig. 1**

The above figure connected two adjacent patterns of the G major scale with a half-step slide. Continuing this process, we can slide again to extend the range even more:

**Fig. 2**

Now try the same concept using a whole-step slide on a different string:

**Fig. 3**

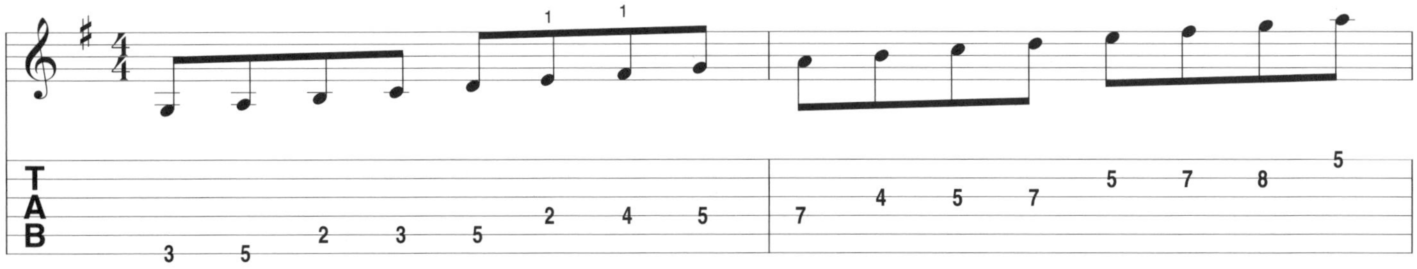

Now try this example, which uses slides in the major pentatonic scale:

**Fig. 4**

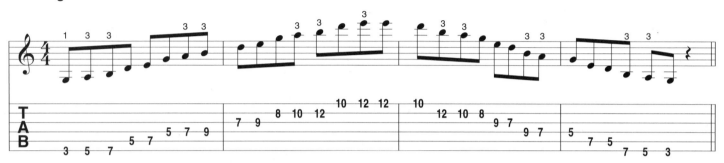

As you can see, this increases the amount of fingerboard you can cover. Ultimately, the player wants to be able to perform these moves unconsciously, but for now practice the scales with these set slide locations. We recommend practicing using the slide to connect adjacent scale patterns, gradually connecting the entire neck. Practice inserting half-step and whole-step slides on different strings.

## Changing Positions Using Stretching

As you can see from the previous examples, the three note-per-string scale patterns already cover a couple of positions. These scale patterns are good for changing positions and as a "go between" for the basic five patterns. The concept of stretching will have the player executing four notes on a string. This next example connects pattern 4 (G major) to pattern 5 by playing four notes on the fourth string:

**Fig. 5**

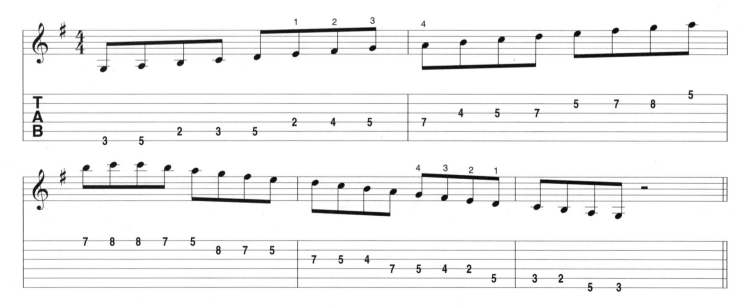

Using this movement again on the second string will shift into a higher position:

**Fig. 6**

These four-note-on-a-string fingerings are quite a stretch. However, they do cover a lot of ground quickly. This next example also uses a stretch, but within the major pentatonic scale, and with three notes on a string:

**Fig. 7**

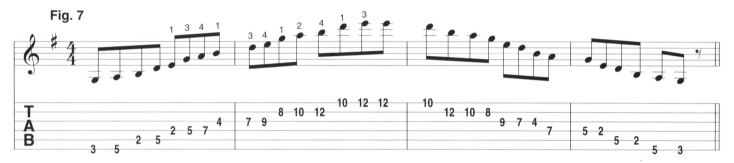

Practice using four notes on a string to connect adjacent major scale patterns and three notes on a string to connect major pentatonic patterns.

## EXERCISE 2

Use this short exercise to become comfortable with combining stretching and a major scale "diatonic thirds" sequence ascending in triplets.

# Changing positions using Position Shifting

Position shifting involves moving the hand to a different position on the neck using a different finger. This technique differs from stretching in that the fretting hand retains the "one finger-a-fret" shape and moves the entire hand to a new location, rather than spreading out the fingers to cover more ground. These are used when covering a wider range. This next example moves from pattern 4 of G major to pattern 1 of the same scale by shifting on the fourth string from a G note with the fourth finger to an A note on the same string with the first finger:

**Fig. 8**

These seem to be the most difficult actions to perform accurately. One must get a sense of the distance the fretting hand is moving to perform these shifts without looking at the fingerboard. This next figure uses the same shift with a major pentatonic scale and connects pattern 1 of D major to pattern 3:

**Fig. 9**

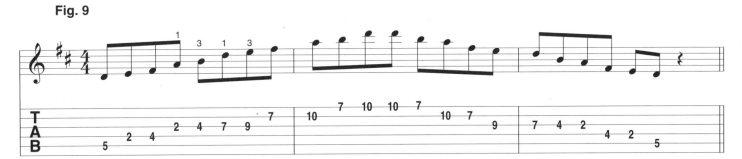

Practice position shifting by connecting patterns that are two patterns apart (pattern 4 to pattern 1, pattern 2 to pattern 4, pattern 1 to pattern 3, pattern 3 to pattern 5, and pattern 5 to pattern 2). Try to do this shifting on different strings. Let this take time. Focus on one or two of these shifting drills every one or two weeks.

This chapter explained the three basic ways to change position on the neck with scale patterns. The next lesson will use these techniques while mixing up the notes in phrases, motifs, and licks. Spend this time practicing each of the three ways to change positions on the neck. Make sure you have at least two ways to perform each of the techniques presented.

Practice these three techniques over any of the major tonality progressions on the play-a-long CD.

**14** **Chapter 14 Chord Progression**

This is a 4/4 straight rock groove with the I, IV, and V chords in E minor.

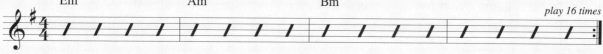

---

## Chapter 14 Lick

Let the open strings sustain in this lick, for a bell-like sound. Make sure you execute the fretted notes cleanly as you s-t-r-e-t-c-h your fingers. Try this over the chapter 14 chord progression.

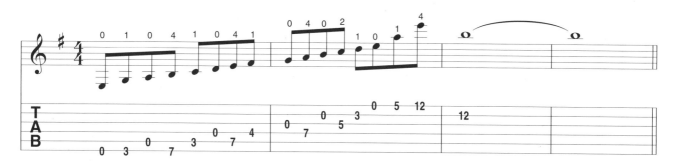

---

| Chapter Fourteen | REVIEW |
| --- | --- |

1. Be able to explain the three ways to change positions on the fingerboard, and why it's important to do so.

2. Be able to play examples demonstrating sliding.

3. Be able to play examples demonstrating stretching.

4. Be able to play examples demonstrating position shifting.

# Three-Octave Scales

## Objectives

- To continue connecting up the neck using:

    1. Sliding

    2. Stretching

    3. Position shifting.

- To introduce three-octave scales.

- To learn lines that change position.

### EXERCISE 1: Technique Exercise

This technique exercise is a good one for covering a large distance along the fretboard, and it (like all of our previous technique exercises) can be adapted and changed to create dozens of other variations. Try this exercise with hammer-ons, pull-offs, triplets, eighth and sixteenth note rhythms, add a new note, invert the shapes, etc. This exercise consists of a tonic, ninth, minor third, diminished fifth, augmented fifth and sixth intervals repeating in a symmetrical pattern. You may want to play the first pattern (starting on F) over an F7#9 chord....it works. We will explore this kind of sound in later chapters; for now you should focus on accuracy of execution and economy of motion.

## Three Octave Scales

Using all three possible methods of shifting up and down the neck, it is possible to play a three-octave scale. Each of the examples below demonstrates a different way to play this scale. Examine each example slowly, making note of where the slides, stretches, or position shifts are located:

**Fig. 1**

with whole-step slides:

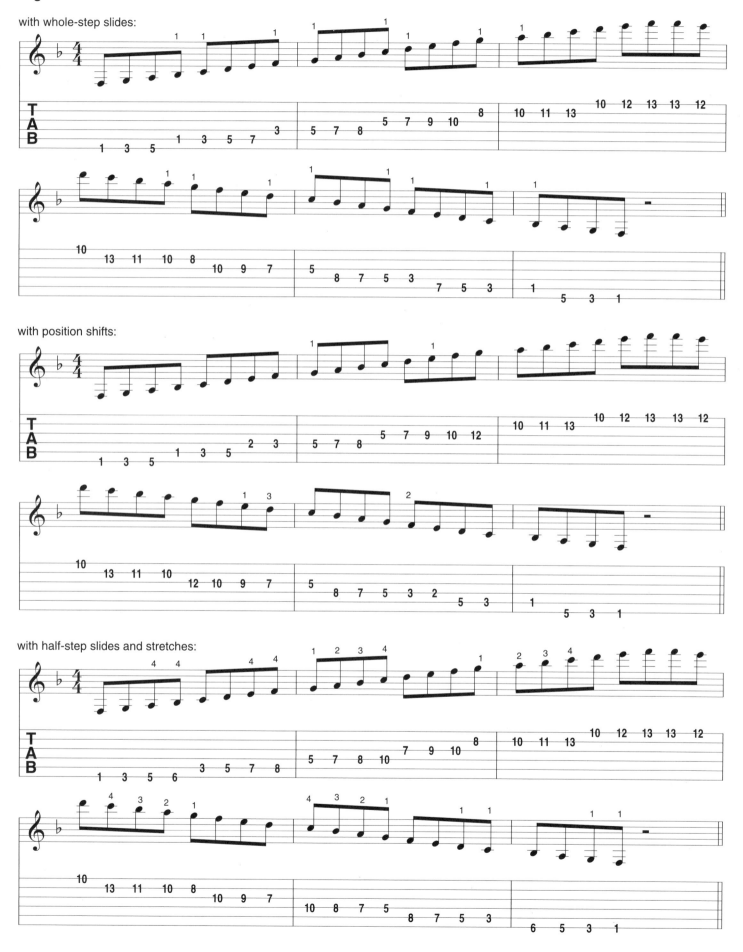

with position shifts:

with half-step slides and stretches:

Practice these very slowly. The idea isn't to race up and down the three-octave scale, but to incorporate the shifting concepts into your own lines. This scale merely shows the possibilities. Practice with different picking methods as well.

# Lines that Change Position

All of these examples demonstrate the three ways to change position. Play them over the suggested chords, and then apply them to any of the play-a-long progressions up to this point:

**Fig. 2**

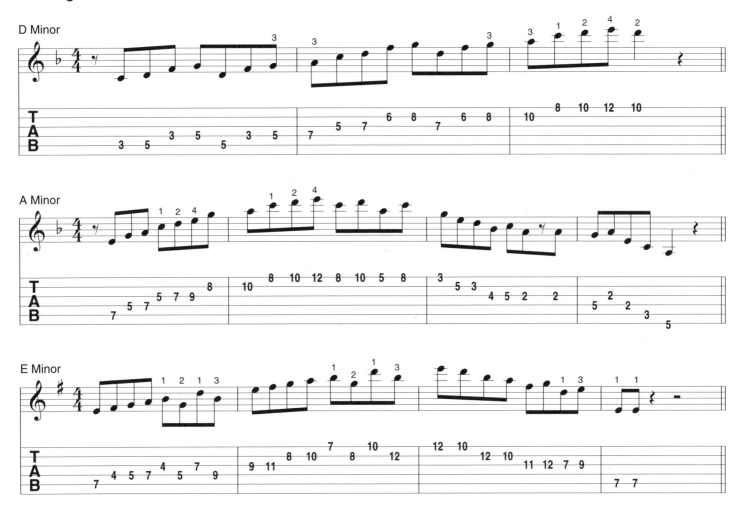

Again, after learning these lines, use hammer-ons, pull-offs, vibrato, etc.

Apply these lines to any of the play-a-long progressions. Try them in different keys and patterns. Remember that all these items are part of the long term practice as well. Don't expect to be a master of changing position on the fingerboard after two weeks. Make position shifting a part of your practice routine.

**Chapter 15 Chord Progression**

## Chapter 15 Lick

Use this lick over the Chapter 15 chord progression

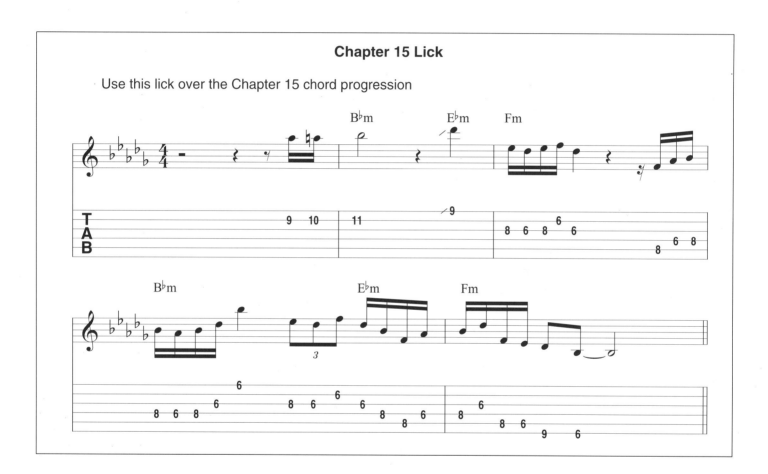

| Chapter Fifteen | **REVIEW** |
|---|---|

1. Be able to play a three-octave scale using the examples given or one of your own design.

2. Be able to play the given lines that change position.

3. Be able to change position while improvising over any of the play-a-long progressions.

# Chromaticism and Passing Tones

## Objectives

- To add chromaticism to lines.

- To add passing tones to the major and minor scales.

- To add passing tones to three note-per-string patterns.

### EXERCISE 1: Technique Exercise

The technique exercise for this chapter works on the different possibilities for picking and right/left hand coordination. You can use this exercise to work out any "bugs in the system" when it comes to synchronization.

1. Start one cycle with a downpick from C; notice how the pick moves "inside" from one string to the other.

2. Start another cycle with an upstroke from C; the pick moves "outside" when you change from the B string back to the E string.

3. Play with hammer-ons and pull-offs.

Work this exercise up to your top speed!

## Basic Use of Chromaticism

Up until now, our lines have consisted of scalar and arpeggiated movement. These two types of movement can be combined with the use of short chromatic phrases to lend an even more interesting contour (and sound) to our lines. The use of these short chromatic phrases adds a "smoothness" to one's lines.

*Chromaticism,* for our immediate purposes, will consist of using a series of half steps in a row between scale or arpeggio tones, as passing tones. This is not the end-all discussion of chromaticism, merely one technique that is easy to use immediately.

## Adding Chromatic Passing Tones to the Major and Minor Scales

The following examples demonstrate this. Extend each of the following to the full range of at least two scale patterns. Here are two possibilities for the major scale:

**Fig. 1**

Here are some phrases that demonstrate this sound:

**Fig. 2**

C Major

Let's try adding passing tones in the minor scale:

**Fig. 3**

Here are some phrases demonstrating this sound:

**Fig. 4**

A Minor

A Minor

The rhythmic placement of these chromatic tones is important. When the chromatic tone is placed on a downbeat, the listener will notice its slight dissonance more than if the chromatic tone is on an upbeat.

**EXERCISE 2**

The following short ideas (motifs) are examples of chromatic passing tones in a number of combinations. These can also be called upper and/or lower neighbor tones, or "targeting" of a diatonic note by using surrounding chromatic notes. Our diatonic note is the chord tone C. You can use this approach with any strong diatonic note (a chord tone) that fits the chord you are playing over.

Try these over any "C type" chord (C tonic)—C9 with a Funk feel, a C major triad with an eighth-note Rock feel, a Cmaj7 with a Bossa Nova feel, or a C minor triad with a Pop groove.

In the space provided, write some short motifs of your own:

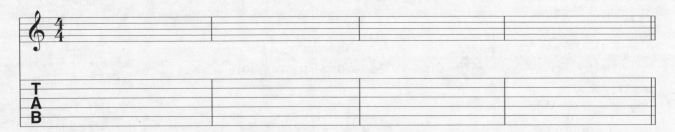

# Adding Passing Tones to the Three Note-per-String Scale Patterns

Let's add these passing tones to the three note-per-string scale patterns in a random fashion. Play each of the following phrases:

**Fig. 5**

The three note-per-string patterns seem to make the fingering of these passing tones a bit easier. Do you hear the smoothness that the chromatic passing tones add? Using any of the play-a-long progressions, apply this technique whether you're using three notes-per-string or the basic patterns. Of course, use all performance techniques.

**Chapter 16 Lick**

This idea uses chromaticism as a way to build interest for the listener (especially in the second measure). Try this lick over the chapter 16 chord progression.

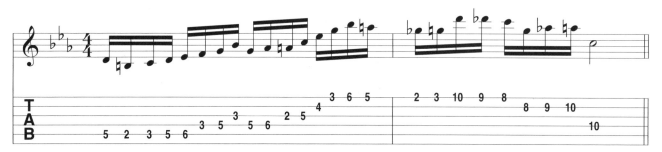

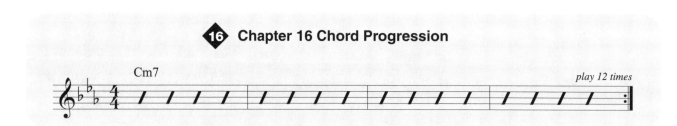

**Chapter 16 Chord Progression**

| Chapter Sixteen | **REVIEW** |

1. Be able to play two patterns of the major and minor scales using passing tones.

2. Be able to play the given examples demonstrating this technique.

3. Be able to play three note-per-string patterns with passing tones added.

4. Be able to play the examples given.

# Key Center Playing

## Objectives

- To explain key center playing in major tonality.
- To use key center playing over progressions which utilize seventh chord harmonies.
- To use key center playing over progressions which utilize triad harmonies.

### EXERCISE 1: Stretching Exercise (1 minute)

Place your hand on a tabletop so that it is flat—with all fingers and the thumb making contact with the table. Slowly raise your index (first) finger *while keeping the other fingers on the tabletop.* Raise the finger to the point of maximum extension, hold the position for a couple seconds, and then slowly lower it back to the tabletop. Follow this procedure for each finger of the right hand, and then repeat the process with the left hand.

## Key Center Playing in Major Tonality

*Key center playing* provides a way to organize the chords from any progression into simple recognizable segments. This is done by grouping adjacent chords into a key and using that scale to improvise over them. Thinking in this way while playing should make you sound smooth. It is critical that you have a thorough knowledge of the harmonized major scales so these relationships can be seen quickly. Once the player has grouped adjacent chords into key centers, they may use the scale and arpeggios, to create lines. Let's take a look at how this is done.

## Using Key Center Playing over Seventh Chord Progressions in Major Tonality

Look at the following progression:

**Fig. 1**

One way to deduce the key center is to list all the possible keys each of these chords should belong to:

> Gmaj7 – I chord in G, IV chord in D
>
> Em7 – ii chord in D, iii chord in C, vi chord G
>
> Am7 – ii chord in G, iii chord in F, vi chord in C
>
> D7 – V chord in G

Now, looking at this you can see the one common key for all of these is G. This reveals one tip when improvising over major tonality chord progressions: find the dominant chord, and this usually will be the V chord in the key of the proper scale. The method of thinking of all the possible scales these chords can belong to is also a good method as long as it can be done quickly. Of course the best way is to play the chords and hear the key! This will happen with experience. (Meaning, countless repetition of hundreds of songs!)

The next example is a solo over this chord progression. It uses the scale and some arpeggio tones:

**Fig. 2**

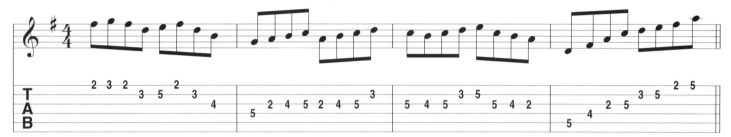

### EXERCISE 2

In the space provided write your own example over the previous chord progression:

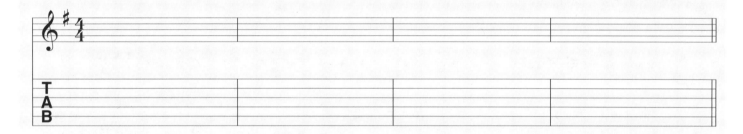

# Using Key Center Playing over Triad Chord Progressions in Major Tonality

**17** **Chapter 17 Chord Progression**

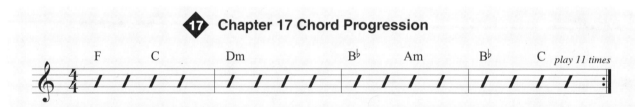

### EXERCISE 3

In progressions that use triadic harmony, deducing the key center may take a couple of seconds longer as there isn't a dominant chord. Take a look at the chapter 17 chord progression and in the spaces provided write down all the possible keys that these chords could belong to. Then, find the key center:

**F:**

**C:**

**Dm:**

**B♭:**

**Am:**

Play the chord progression and listen to its tendencies. Can you hear the key center? Try to sing the note that the chords seem to revolve around. After a while you will be able to hear the key center. Also, the player develops a repertoire of progressions that will never have to be analyzed again. Now play the following study. Several different performance techniques have been notated in this example:

**Chapter 17 Lick**

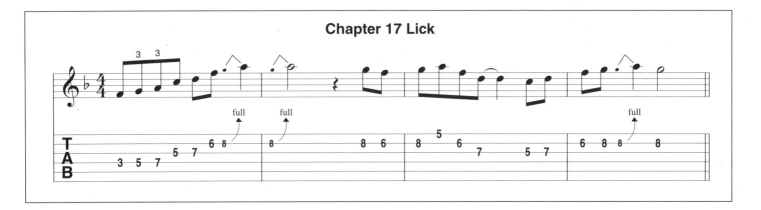

## EXERCISE 4

In the space provided, write your own study over the given progression. Notate all performance techniques used:

Improvise over these progressions using key center thinking. Employ all the devices that have been covered. Make music with all of these tools!

| Chapter Seventeen | REVIEW |
|---|---|

1. Understand the concept of key center playing.

2. Be able to deduce the key center of major tonality chord progressions that use seventh chords or triads.

3. Be able to play the given examples over the progression.

4. Be able to play the self composed examples.

5. Be able to improvise over the given progression.

# Modulation

## 18

## Objective

- To improvise over progressions that modulate (change key centers).

### EXERCISE 1: Technique Exercise

The following exercise provides you the opportunity to develop your technique (accurate interval skips) and have a useful tool for improvising based on the major scale. There are many variations of this type of exercise using diatonic interval leaps. We have presented one exercise in this chapter; more exercises will be studied in later chapters.

Exercise 1 goes through G major scale pattern 4 in diatonic sixth intervals using alternate picking in one position:

## Improvising over Modulating Key Centers

Up to this point we have been improvising over progressions that remained in one key. The progressions in this chapter's lesson will change key centers (the changing of keys in a song is known as *modulation*). Let's examine two chord progressions that use modulation. This first progression is actually the exact same chord sequence in two keys.

**Fig. 1**

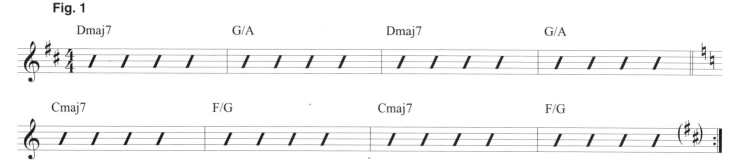

Notice that the entire progression was moved down a whole step. One of the most important ways to sound smooth over these kinds of progressions is to find the scales in the same position on the neck (or as close to it as you can get). This next example can be played entirely in second position. It works over the previous chord progression.

**Fig. 2**

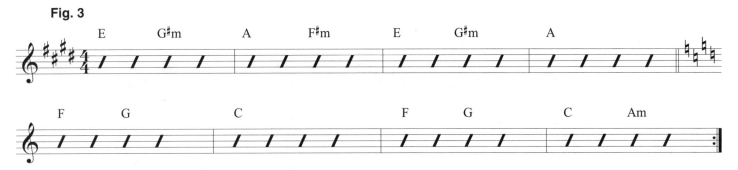

Notice how you were using pattern 1 for the D major measures and pattern 2 for the C major measures. Now try playing the example in fourth and fifth position. This will require pattern 2 for D major and pattern 3 for C major.

When playing over progressions that modulate (change key) *try to get the scale patterns in the same position.* This will make the transitions from one key to the next much smoother. Let's look at another chord progression.

This example uses two different chord sequences that change keys abruptly.

**Fig. 3**

| E | G♯m | A | F♯m | E | G♯m | A |
| --- | --- | --- | --- | --- | --- | --- |

| F | G | C | F | G | C | Am |
| --- | --- | --- | --- | --- | --- | --- |

This progression is in two keys—E major for four measures and C major for four measures. Try playing the following study in fourth and fifth position, then sixth and seventh position (the TAB has been left out to make this less confusing):

Practice improvising over each of these progressions using the closest possible scale patterns. Try different feels and tempos. Once you feel comfortable with changing patterns, add all performance techniques. Many of the examples use straight eighth notes for physical training purposes. However, musically you must mix up the rhythms of your phrases! More on this later.

## Chapter 18 Lick

Try this over the chapter 18 chord progression.

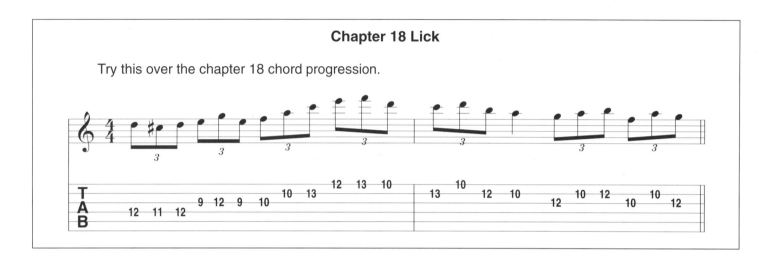

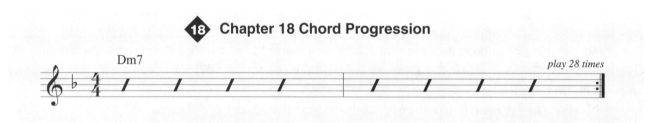

**Chapter 18 Chord Progression**

---

| **Chapter Eighteen** | **REVIEW** |
|---|---|

1. Be able to play and record the two given progressions.

2. Be able to play the given melodic studies in two different positions each.

3. Be able to improvise over the progressions using the closest scale patterns.

# The Blues

## Objectives

- To begin a study of the blues tonality.

- To learn the construction and patterns of the blues scale.

- To learn blues scale phrases.

- To learn two standard twelve-bar blues chord progressions.

- To improvise over a standard twelve-bar blues progression using the blues scale and blues phrases.

---

### EXERCISE 1: Creativity Exercise

Go ahead and sing a lick (musical idea) and then try to play it! You'll probably be a little uncomfortable at first; the point is *not* to be a great singer. Your ears are more sophisticated than your hands are. You've probably been listening to music all your life! You can begin to play the way that you dream of playing (how you really *hear* it), if you try this exercise. Keep it short (you are creating licks, not symphonies). *Warning! This can vastly improve your playing!!!*

---

## The Blues Tonality

The blues tonality (in its simplest form) is a combination of major and minor tonalities. Blues harmony is based on the I, IV, and V chords of the major tonality. However, the chords are all dominant (seventh chords) in quality. The scales that are used to improvise over these chords contain minor thirds (not in all cases) and the addition of the lowered fifth degree. This combination (used with call and response) yields the plaintive, crying effect of the blues. This is an overly simplified approach, but it gets the student started in the right direction. In reality, blues is less about scales and more about feeling. We use scales and other devices as mere tools to try and achieve these sounds. We will use the blues scale, its variations, and other scales to improvise over blues-based progressions.

## The Blues Scale

The blues scale, as most players know it, is based on the minor pentatonic scale with the addition of the lowered fifth:

| **C Minor Pentatonic Scale:** | C | E♭ | F | | G | B♭ | C |
|---|---|---|---|---|---|---|---|
| | 1 | 3 | 4 | | 5 | 7 | 1(8) |
| **C Blues Scale:** | C | E♭ | F | G♭ | G | B♭ | C |
| | 1 | 3 | 4 | ♭5 | 5 | 7 | 1(8) |

The following example shows patterns 4 and 2 of the blues scale. A suggested fingering is shown on the accompanying fretboard diagrams:

**Fig. 1**

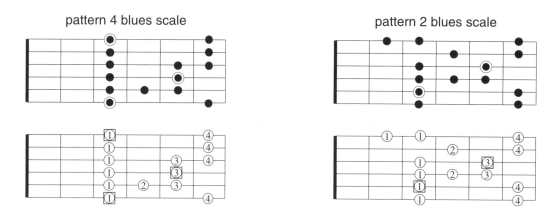

pattern 4 blues scale          pattern 2 blues scale

Practice these scales in the same fashion as all previously learned scales. (Begin on the lowest tonic up to the highest note using different keys, different positions, alternate picking, hammer-ons, pull-offs, etc.) Up to this point diatonic scale sequencing was one device used to help mix up the notes of the scales to produce melodies, however, this technique doesn't work as well for the blues scale. A more useful approach is to learn blues scale phrases.

# Blues Scale Phrases

The following phrases demonstrate the sound of the blues. Learn to play each of these phrases in the positions and patterns notated, then practice them in different keys, patterns, and positions:

**Fig. 2 – C Blues**

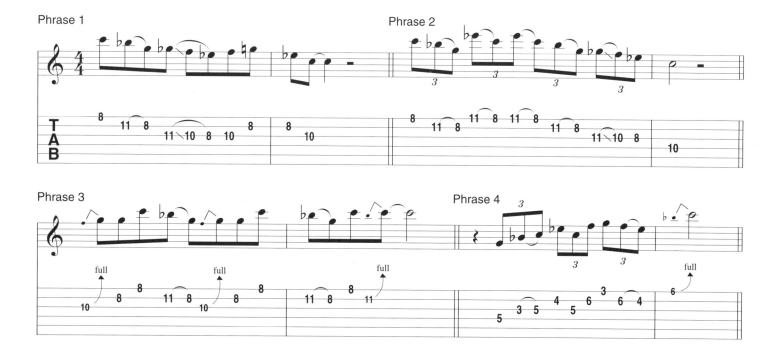

Notice which notes are bent in the preceding figures. Concentrate on bending the seventh and the fourth degree of each scale pattern. Focus on the accurate intonation of your bends.

# Blues Chord Progressions

As stated earlier, blues harmony is based on the I, IV, and V chords of a given key. These chords are all dominant in chord quality. (There are also minor blues progressions, these will discussed in upcoming chapters.) The twelve-bar blues progression is a standard format in this style. The next figure shows two twelve-bar blues progressions in the key of C.

**Fig. 3**

**Quick change progression**

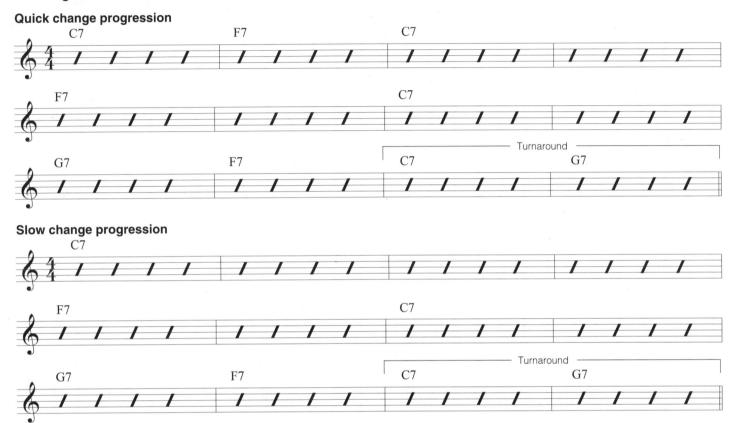

**Slow change progression**

Note the difference in the preceding progressions. In the first progression, the IV chord appears in the second measure. This is called a "quick change," while the second progression is called a "slow change" (the IV chord appearing in the fifth measure). The last two measures of a blues progression are called the *turnaround.* There are different kinds of turnarounds. Let's just use a simple I chord for a measure and a V chord for a measure for now.

# Improvising over Blues Chord Progressions

Begin your blues improvising by using some of the blues phrases given earlier on. For now it's important to keep your phrases short and repeat them often. Think of blues songs that you have heard. Notice how the lyrics have a repeating theme (often called "call and response"):

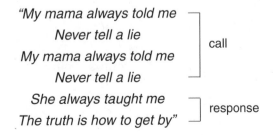

*"My mama always told me*
*Never tell a lie*
*My mama always told me*
*Never tell a lie*  — call

*She always taught me*
*The truth is how to get by"*  — response

Try to do this in your improvisations. It is an excellent way to make your playing accessible to the listener. Experiment with this over the given chord progression for this chapter.

## Chapter 19 Lick

This idea uses the A blues scale. Use this lick over the chapter 19 chord progression. Play with "straight eighths" and a shuffle feel.

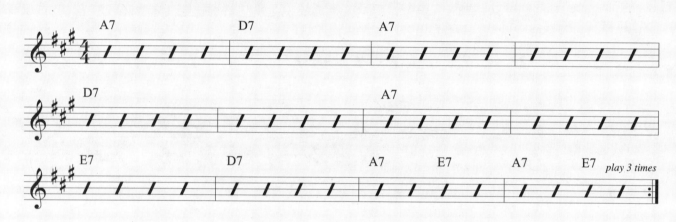

### Chapter 19 Chord Progression

This is a "quick-change" blues in A.

| Chapter Nineteen | **REVIEW** |
| --- | --- |

1.  Understand basic blues tonality.

2.  Understand quick and slow change twelve-bar blues progressions.

3.  Be able to play a two-octave blues scale in two patterns in any key.

4.  Be able to play the blues phrases given in any key.

5.  Be able to improvise over the given chord progression for this chapter.

# Blues Variations

## 20

## Objectives

- To learn a variation of the blues scale.
- To learn more blues scale phrases.
- To learn and use "call and response" in blues improvising.
- To learn more blues progressions.
- To combine all materials over a blues progression.

### EXERCISE 1: Technique Exercise

This exercise is another diatonic interval leap study similar to the exercise in chapter 18. It goes through G major scale pattern 4 in diatonic fifth intervals using alternate picking in one position:

## Blues Scale Variation

The following blues scale variation uses the natural sixth degree in place of the seventh. It gives a more "major" sound to blues scale phrases. Here are its notes from a C tonic:

| C Blues Scale: | C | E♭ | F | G♭ | G | A | C |
|---|---|---|---|---|---|---|---|
| | 1 | 3 | 4 | ♭5 | 5 | 6 | 1(8) |

This is not an "official" scale. However, it gets the student creating more realistic blues sounds. Here's patterns 4 and 2 for this blues scale variation:

**Fig. 1**   pattern 4 blues scale variation                    pattern 2 blues scale variation

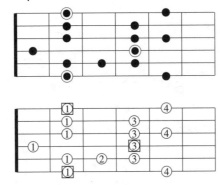
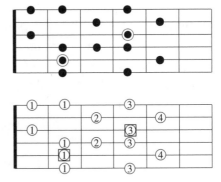

Try not to look at this as an entirely new scale. It's merely changing one note of the already familiar blues scale. Be able to play these scale patterns in any key.

# More Blues Scale Phrases

Here are some more blues scale phrases in C. Some of them use the blues scale variation. Play these in their designated positions, then move them to different keys and patterns:

**Fig. 2**

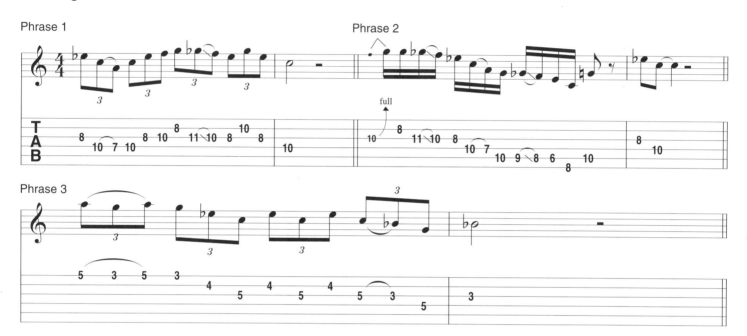

# Call and Response

"Call and response" is one of the most important aspects of blues tonality improvising. It's a very simple device yet extremely effective in keeping the listener's attention. Play the following example for C blues:

**Fig. 3**

Do you hear the effect? The first phrase asks a question, the second phrase answers it. The "question" phrase ends on a pitch other than the tonic, while the "answer" phrase ends on the tonic. That's call and response. This is an over simplified approach but it gets the player making sense to the listener quickly because it's very "conversational." Once you can apply this concept, use it while resolving to notes other than the tonic. Practice this with a partner by having them play the "call" and you play the "response." Use one- or two-measure phrases and switch roles frequently.

# More Blues Progressions

In chapter 19 we focused on twelve-bar blues progressions that used either a slow or a quick change. In this chapter we will introduce a sixteen-bar and an eight-bar blues progression.

Be able to play and improvise over these progressions in any key. There are an infinite number of blues progressions. Each song has its own nuances. Eleven, thirteen, fifteen, and twenty-four-bar blues progressions are common. Be flexible in your approach to these songs and listen!

**Fig. 4**

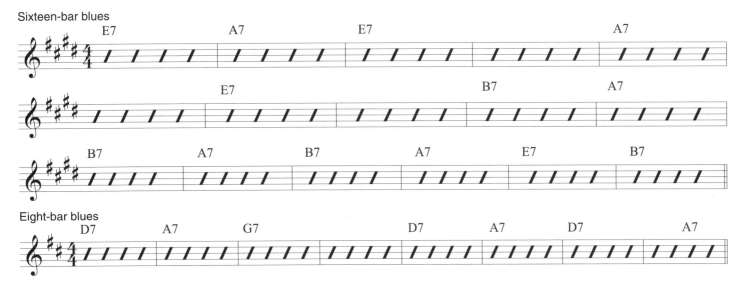

# Combining Major and Minor Pentatonics with the Blues Scale, and its Variation

As was stated earlier, blues tonality is a combination of major and minor. Let's continue this process by using the major and minor pentatonics with the blues scale and the blues scale variation. We will do this in a mechanical fashion by using a twelve-bar blues and inserting different scales at different places. All scales are from the tonic of the key center. The next example is a single chorus of a twelve-bar blues solo over a quick change in the key of C:

**Fig. 5**

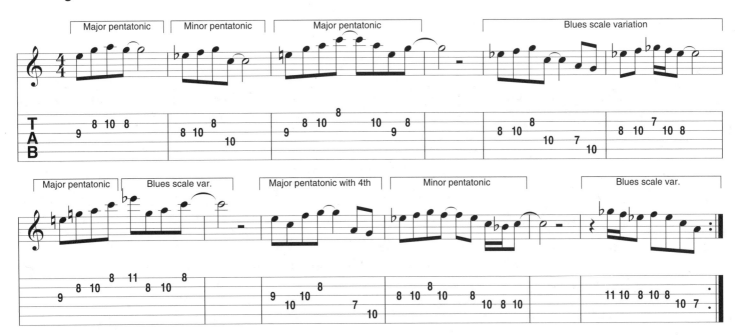

The use of the different scales gives a more interesting flavor to the blues. Actually, it's more desirable to think of using other notes than scales, but this method forces the improviser to choose these other notes. Notice the use of scales that contain the minor third of the key center over the IV chord (F7 in this particular example), and the major third over the I and V chords. Try this on your own using the suggested scales and their placement above.

## Chapter 20 Lick

Try this over the chapter 20 chord progression

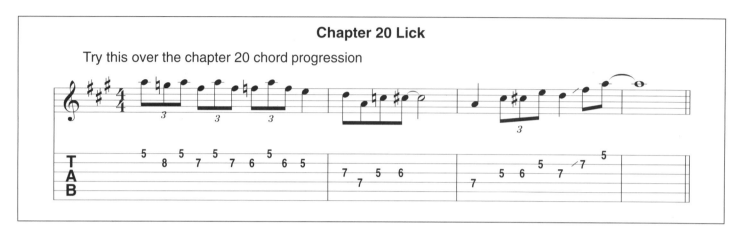

## 20  Chapter 20 Chord Progression

This is a "slow-change" twelve-bar blues in A

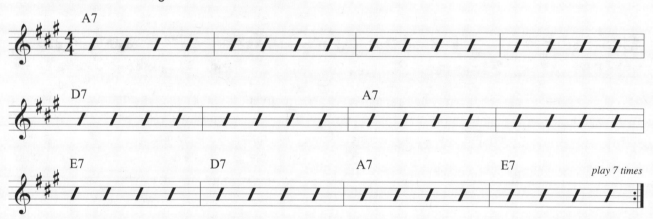

| Chapter Twenty | **REVIEW** |
| --- | --- |

1. Be able to construct the blues scale variation on any tonic.

2. Be able to play two patterns of the blues scale variation in any key.

3. Be able to play the given blues phrases.

4. Be able to mix up major and minor pentatonics with the blues scale and its variation, over blues progressions.

# Minor Blues

## 21

## Objectives

- To learn a variation of the minor pentatonic scale.
- To learn a minor blues progression and be able to improvise over it.
- To learn to use bends of a minor or major triad.

**EXERCISE 1: Stretching Exercise (1 minute)**

This chapter's stretch should be performed after any other basic warm-up stretch (see previous chapters). Some of the best slow stretches are achieved by using chord shapes on the guitar by holding the chords in place as you relax and breathe, oxygenating the muscles and giving your fretting hand a strong stretch. The important thing is to not overdo this stretch. *Never strain, or hold to the point of pain!* Here we go:

- Hold this chord shape (C major add9) for 10 seconds. Feel free to strum the chord as you hold the chord. Remember that your focus is on relaxing your hand, *not* rhythm guitar!

- Switch to this chord shape next: (F major add9). Hold for 10 seconds.

Continue to increase the intensity of the stretch by moving down a whole step; to the sixth fret. You will play the same two chord shapes as before, but now the spacing is wider. Move again to the third fret, and repeat the chord shapes. Then go to the second fret and repeat again. Finally, if you'd like to have the maximum possible stretch, play the two chord shapes in first position (the first fret).

## Minor Pentatonic Scale Variation

This variation of the minor pentatonic scale is a simple one: merely add the ninth (or second) degree of the minor scale to the minor pentatonic in both octaves. The spelling and the notes in the key of C minor are:

| C | D | E♭ | F | G | B♭ | C |
|---|---|-----|---|---|-----|---|
| 1 | 2 | (♭)3 | 4 | 5 | (♭)7 | 1(8) |

With the following fretboard and fingering diagrams, play patterns 2 and 4 for this minor pentatonic scale variation. Try not to look at this as a whole new scale—see it as something familiar with a note added. (Exactly what it is!):

**Fig. 1**      pattern 4 blues scale variation

pattern 2 blues scale variation

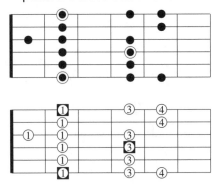

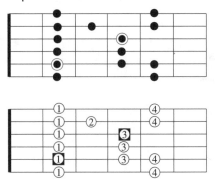

# Minor Blues Progression

Blues progressions based on major or dominant chords have been used up to this point. Let's look at a twelve-bar blues progression in the key of A minor:

**Fig. 2**

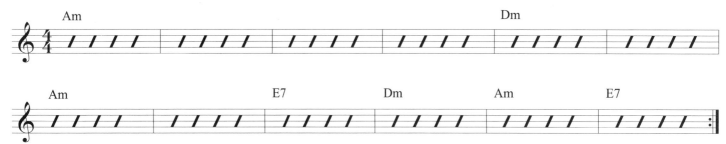

This progression should look familiar. The only difference is that the i and iv chords are minor instead of major or dominant. There are also minor blues progressions that use a minor V chord or mix up the use of the minor and dominant V chords. This next minor blues progression uses a dominant V chord and introduces the use of the VI chord of the minor scale:

**Fig. 3**

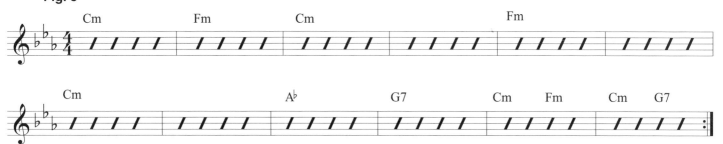

Notice the feeling the VI chord gives. It delays the arrival of the V chord, then the V chord pushes toward resolving to the i chord. As mentioned previously, there are endless variations of minor blues progressions. Be flexible and listen! Practice improvising on each of the progressions above, after you have learned the proper tools from the next section.

# Improvising over Minor Blues Progressions

Soloing or improvising over minor blues progressions is not that much different from major blues progressions though there are a couple of things to mention. Obviously, previous blues progressions flirted with the use of the major third of the key center while the i chord was being sounded. This will be avoided when improvising over minor blues progressions. The use of the regular blues scale, minor pentatonic, and the minor scale will be more important here. The use of the minor pentatonic variation will add some additional color here as well. Learn the following twelve-bar minor blues solo. Analyze the note choices. The solo uses the chords from the second progression.

**Fig. 4**

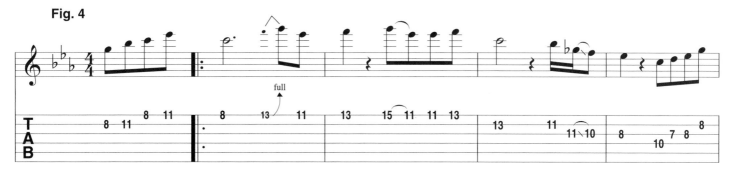

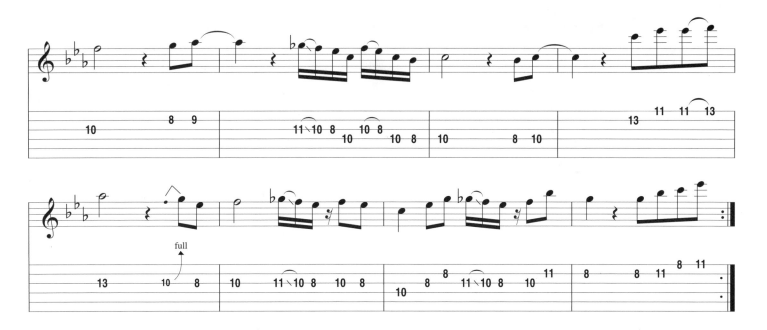

## EXERCISE 2

In the space provided below, write your own study. Begin by using only eighth notes; use all previously studied scales and arpeggios. After you have played this a couple times, add your own articulations: slides, hammer-ons, pull-offs, remove some notes, vibrato, bends, change the rhythms!!!! Make it musical!

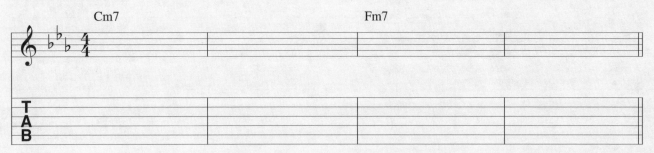

# Major and Minor Third Bends

Bending is an important aspect of blues-based improvising. Bending up a major or minor third is a special attention-getting device.

**Fig. 5**

In the key of A minor try bending the A note up a minor third:

Now try bending the C note up a major third:

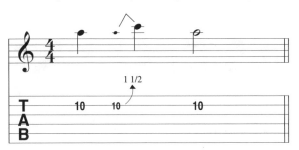 

(Note: you'll really have to hook your thumb over the top of the neck so the bending finger has something to push against!)

In A minor this means you're bending the tonic (A) up a minor third, and the third of the key center (C) up a major third. Try to find other notes of the key which, when bent up a minor or major third, will produce a note of the A minor or A blues tonality. Learn and play the following blues licks that utilize this technique:

**Fig. 6**

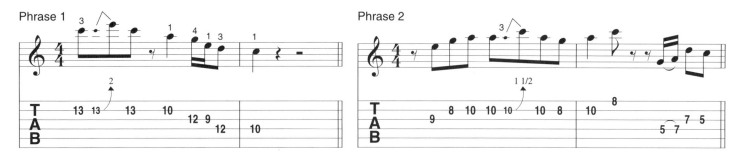

Practice these ideas in different positions using different strings. Start by using the third finger of your fretting hand to bend, then try other finger combinations. Both of these lines work over an A minor chord.

---

### Chapter 21 Lick

This lick will work over Fig. 3. It will also work over non-blues minor progressions like the chapter 21 chord progression.

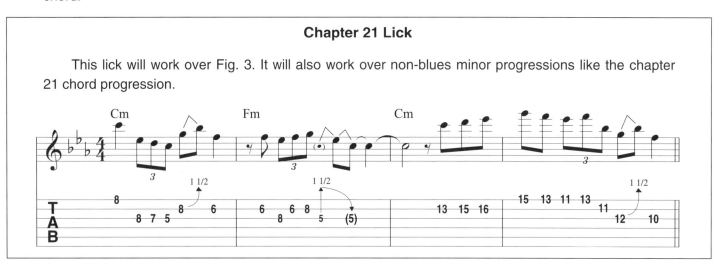

---

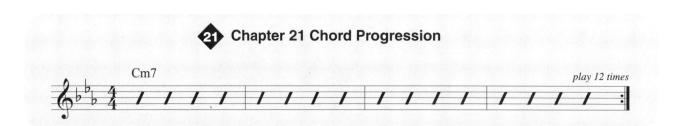

**21** **Chapter 21 Chord Progression**

---

**Chapter Twenty-One**          **REVIEW**

1.  Be able to play 2 patterns of the minor pentatonic scale variation in any key.

2.  Be able to play the minor blues progressions and the given minor blues solo.

3.  Be able to improvise over a minor blues progression, using the proper scales.

4.  Be able to use major and minor third bends in minor and major blues progressions.

# The Dorian Scale

## Objectives

- To learn the construction of the Dorian scale and its application in chord progressions.

- To learn patterns of the Dorian scale.

- To learn Dorian scale sequences and motifs.

- To combine Dorian scale movement with previously learned materials over chord progressions.

### EXERCISE 1: Technique Exercise

This is another exercise with diatonic interval leaps. It goes through the G major scale in diatonic sixth intervals using alternate picking, moving up the fretboard on the E and G strings, with additional variations.

## The Dorian Scale

The Dorian scale is a very widely used sound. Its construction is based on raising the sixth degree of a natural minor scale:

| C | D | E♭ | F | G | A | B♭ | C |
|---|---|-----|---|---|---|-----|---|
| 1 | 2 | (♭)3 | 4 | 5 | raised 6 | (♭)7 | 1(8) |

The sound of the Dorian is "brighter" than the natural minor scale. There are many uses for the Dorian scale. It can be found in a lot of modal jazz, as well as in pop, Latin, and blues. The Dorian scale is also one of the *modes* of the major scale. It is the second mode of the major scale—that is, the scale of C major, but starting and ending on the D note. Some see this as an easier method of learning the modes of the major scale. The approach we use is to see each of the scales as its own entity, which has its own set of chords and sounds. This allows the player to become familiar with the sounds and tendencies of each of the major scale modes. The classification of major, minor, or blues tonality also helps the player use these scales or modes in the proper harmonic settings. (The Dorian scale is a minor tonality scale.)

The Dorian scale may be used from the root of a minor chord. It should also be used when a IV chord in a minor tonality chord progression is either a major or dominant chord, as in the following progression:

**Fig. 1**

*Key signature denotes C Dorian.

Use the Dorian scale based on the tonic of the key center. The note that was changed in the natural minor to yield the Dorian scale (the raised sixth degree) causes the IV chord of the harmonized scale to be either a major triad, or a dominant chord. Other chords in the harmonized scale change as well, however the major or dominant IV chord is seen quite often and requires the use of the Dorian scale (from the key center tonic) to make the listener "hear" it.

# Patterns of the Dorian Scale

The following diagrams furnish patterns and fingerings for the Dorian scale (patterns 2 and 4):

**Fig. 2**

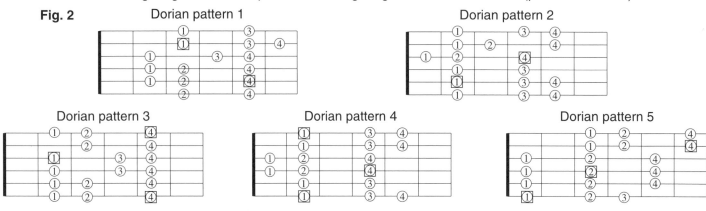

Be able to play these ascending and descending in any key.

# Dorian Scale Sequences and Motifs

As with the previously learned scales, sequences help us to learn the fingering patterns and give ideas on how to combine the notes to make melodies. The following examples show the ascending and descending versions of three sequences. Be able to play each of them ascending and descending through the entire Dorian scale fingering patterns. Always begin with alternate picking, then apply hammer-ons, pull-offs, and all other methods for producing notes:

**Fig. 3 – Dorian sequences**

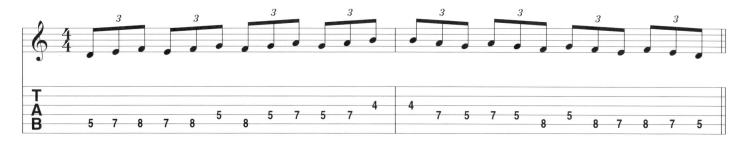

**Fig. 4**

**Fig. 5**

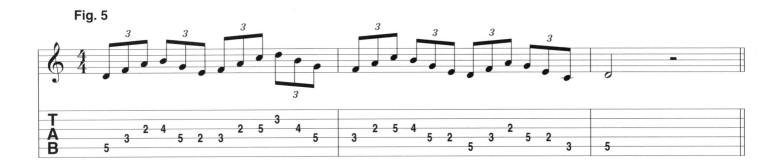

# Combining the Dorian with Other Scales over Chord Progressions

Looking at this scale, one can see how closely it's related to the blues and minor pentatonic scales, as well as the minor pentatonic variation. The Dorian scale may be used in a blues progression wherever you would use these other scales. The important thing is to hear the sound of this scale. The raised sixth degree sounds a bit odd to some players who have not used it before. Play the following twelve-bar blues solo. It uses some note choices from the Dorian and other scales:

**Fig. 6**

The next example combines the Dorian scale with other minor tonality scales over a "vamp" (a repeating progression with one or two chords). This particular vamp uses the i minor chord moving to the IV dominant chord:

**Fig. 7**

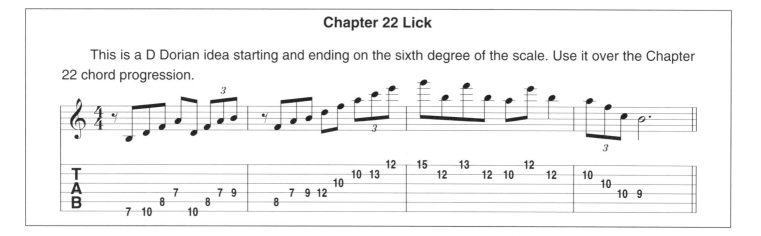

### Chapter 22 Lick

This is a D Dorian idea starting and ending on the sixth degree of the scale. Use it over the Chapter 22 chord progression.

### 22 Chapter 22 Chord Progression

Continue combining all materials over the given chord progression, while retaining your long term goal of knowing all scales in all five patterns on the neck.

Dm7

*play 4 times*

*Key signature denotes D Dorian.

---

**Chapter Twenty-Two**          **REVIEW**

1. Be able to construct the Dorian scale on any tonic.

2. Know where and when to use the Dorian scale.

3. Be able to play the Dorian scale in any key, in two different positions.

4. Be able to play sequences ascending and descending over the entire range of the Dorian scale in two patterns.

5. Be able to play the given motifs in two different keys and patterns.

6. Be able to improvise with the Dorian and other minor tonality scales over the given chord progression.

# 23 The Dorian Scale and Variations

## Objectives

- To learn a variation of the Dorian scale.
- To learn phrases in the Dorian scale.
- To combine Dorian, blues, and minor pentatonic scales.
- To improvise over progressions that combine Dorian and minor scale harmony.

### EXERCISE 1: Technique Exercise

Exercise 1 continues our diatonic interval leap study by going through G major scale pattern 4 in diatonic fourth intervals using alternate picking in one position:

## Dorian Scale Variation

This scale variation is presented to create interest by adding notes to the Dorian scale. This Dorian scale variation simply adds the lowered fifth of the scale to give a "blues" effect to the Dorian scale sound. Use it wherever you would use the Dorian scale. Here is the spelling, and the note choices for this variation:

| C | D | E♭ | F | G♭ | G | A | B♭ | C |
|---|---|-----|---|-----|---|---|-----|---|
| 1 | 2 | (♭)3 | 4 | (♭)5 | 5 | raised 6 | (♭)7 | 1(8) |

Here are patterns 2 and 4 for this variation:

**Fig. 1**

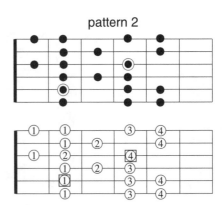

The following two-measure phrases demonstrate the sound of this scale:

**Fig. 2**

# Dorian Scale Phrases

The following phrases use the Dorian scale. These phrases are longer than the previous ones (four measures each).

**Fig. 3**

Try to get a sense of phrasing in two and four measure sections. This will help you construct longer phrases and play the sections of a song.

## EXERCISE 2

Write your idea using the C Dorian scale variation as your source. Use a variety of musical devices to help develop your phrasing, such as repetition, motifs (small note or rhythmic groupings).

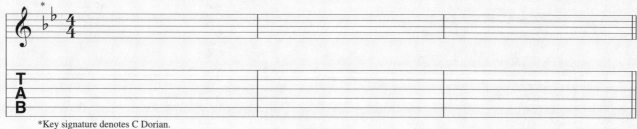

*Key signature denotes C Dorian.

# Combining Dorian, Blues, and Minor Pentatonic Scales

Now let's combine these three scales to make some phrases. These phrases are either two or four measures in length:

**Fig. 4**

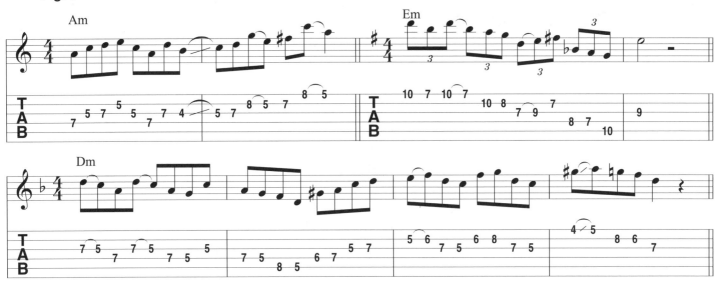

# Progressions that Combine Dorian and Minor Scale Harmony

As was stated in the previous chapter, Dorian scale harmony uses a major, or dominant IV chord. Frequently, you will encounter chord progressions that mix these two scale sounds. We will work with one progression that uses this concept. Play the following progression:

**Fig. 5**

There are several ways to improvise over this progression. This next example sticks strictly with the blues and minor pentatonic scales:

**Fig. 6**

This next example uses the Dorian scale in the first two measures (the IV chord is dominant), then the minor scale for a measure (the F chord is the VI chord of the minor scale), and then returns to the Dorian scale for the last measure:

**Fig. 7**

Can you hear the difference between the two examples? When should the player use one or the other approach? These choices are style and taste driven. It is up to the player to decide on the "flavor" they wish to convey to the listener.

**Chapter 23 Lick**

This idea works over C minor7 (the chapter 23 chord progression). It uses elements of the C Dorian scale variation and some chromatic passing tones.

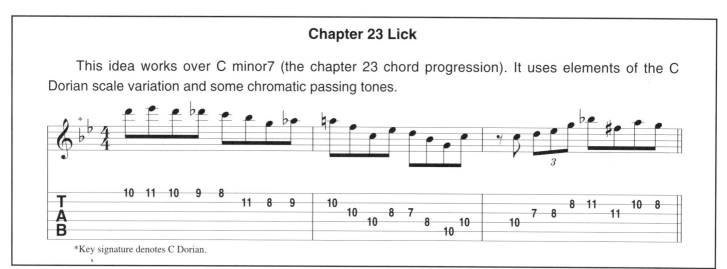

*Key signature denotes C Dorian.

**23** **Chapter 23 Chord Progression**

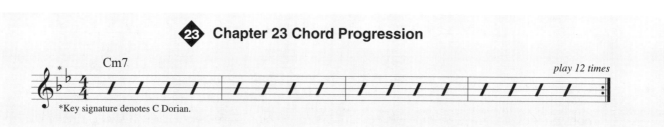

*Key signature denotes C Dorian.

**Chapter Twenty-Three**      **REVIEW**

1. Be able to construct and play the Dorian scale variation in two patterns in any key.

2. Be able to play four-measure phrases with the Dorian scale.

3. Be able to combine Dorian, blues, and minor pentatonic scales.

4. Be able to improvise over progressions that mix Dorian and minor scale harmony.

# The Mixolydian Scale

## 24

## Objectives

- To learn the construction of, and applications for, the Mixolydian scale.
- To learn two patterns of the Mixolydian scale.
- To apply sequences to, and play phrases out of, the Mixolydian scale.
- To improvise with the Mixolydian scale over chord progressions in the blues and major tonalities.

### EXERCISE 1: Creativity Exercise

To expand your musicality, fortify your ear training, and reinforce your ability to find any note on the guitar (that you "hear"); practice singing along with your scales, arpeggios, sequences, and licks as you play them. Your primary goal is not to become a great singer, but is instead to fuse your hands, ears, mind, and creative abilities to help you access the music that you dream about playing!

## The Construction of the Mixolydian Scale

The Mixolydian scale is a major scale with a lowered seventh degree. Since it contains the major third, it can be considered a major, as well as a blues, tonality scale. From a C tonic, the scale would contain the following notes:

| C | D | E | F | G | A | B♭ | C |
|---|---|---|---|---|---|---|---|
| 1 | 2 | 3 | 4 | 5 | 6 | lowered(♭)7 | 1(8) |

The Mixolydian scale is also one of the modes of the major scale; it is the fifth mode. In other words, the D Mixolydian scale contains the same notes as the G major scale. (D is the fifth degree of the G major scale.) Be able to construct this scale from any tonic.

### EXERCISE 2

Do this exercise in pencil!

Fill in the guitar neck below with C major scale patterns 1-5, so that they are laid end to end covering the entire neck with C major shapes. Try to do this without your guitar, using your visualization skills. If this is too difficult to do without your instrument, go ahead and find the shapes on the guitar, and then write out the patterns on the paper.

Now, erase all of the B natural notes (the seventh degree of the scale) and replace them with B♭ notes. You will now have an entire neck diagram of Mixolydian scale patterns. This is a great exercise for your capacity to visualize, and it also helps you to see the Mixolydian scale as a major scale with a lowered seventh. You can also look at it as the fifth mode of a major scale.

# Applications of the Mixolydian scale

The Mixolydian scale has a very unique sound. It can be applied to blues tonality progressions as well as certain major tonality progressions. In the blues tonality, its use should be restricted to the I and V chords, otherwise the major third of the scale would clash with the IV chord:

IV chord in the C blues tonality: F7 Notes: F  A  C  E♭

C Mixolydian scale notes: C  D  E  F  G  A  B♭  C

This is even more clearly demonstrated by playing the following musical example:

**Fig. 1**

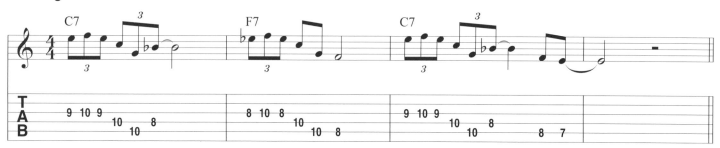

Do you hear how these notes reflect the chord movement? It is very important to note here that the improviser should use scales that contain a minor third (of the key center) over the IV chord in blues tonality progressions. Again, you can use the Mixolydian scale over the I and V chords of blues tonality progressions. There are also certain major tonality progressions the Mixolydian scale may be used over. These progressions use alterations of major tonality progressions which will be discussed in later chapters. In this chapter we will introduce progressions to use the Mixolydian scale over.

# Patterns for the Mixolydian Scale

Here are fingering patterns 2 and 4 for the Mixolydian scale:

**Fig. 2**

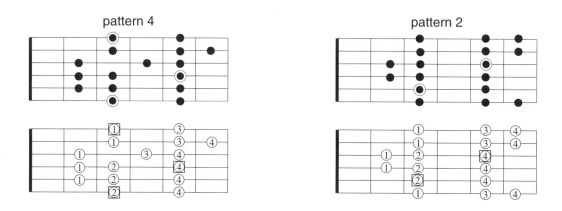

Be able to play these patterns ascending and descending, from any tonic, using alternate picking. Apply hammer-ons and pull-offs as well.

# Sequences and Phrases in the Mixolydian Scale

Apply each of the following sequences to the full range of the Mixolydian scale patterns:

**Fig. 3 – Mixolydian sequences**

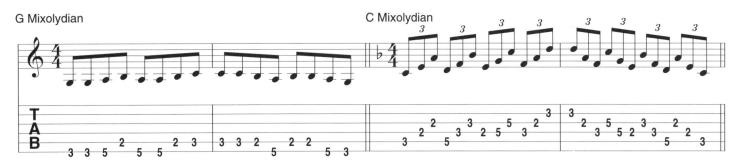

Play each of the following phrases, moving them to other positions (keys) and other patterns (same key):

**Fig. 4 – Mixolydian phrases**

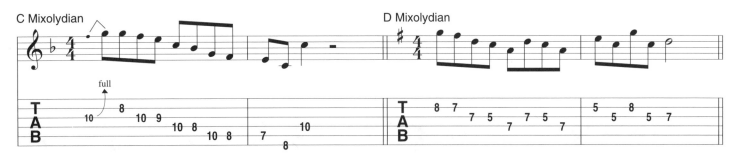

# Improvising with the Mixolydian Scale

We will look at improvising in the blues tonality with the Mixolydian scale in upcoming chapters. For now we will work with some vamps. Besides the suggested play-a-long progression, which is a chord vamp, the following progressions may be used to practice improvising with the Mixolydian scale:

**Fig. 5**

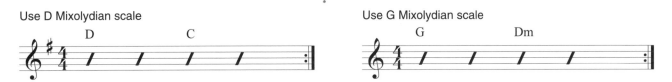

These progressions are based on alterations of the major tonality harmony which will be discussed later. They are introduced here to assist the player in getting these scales and patterns into their playing. Try to "hear" the scale. That is, try to get an overall sense of the kinds of melodies produced by this scale. Use the play-a-long progression as well as the progressions above.

### Chapter 24 Lick

Use this idea over the chapter 24 chord progression. It uses elements of the D Mixolydian and D blues scales.

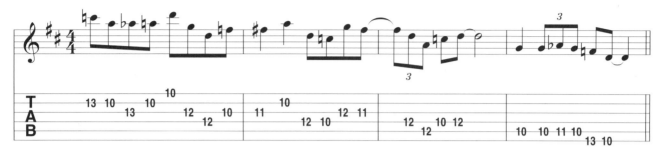

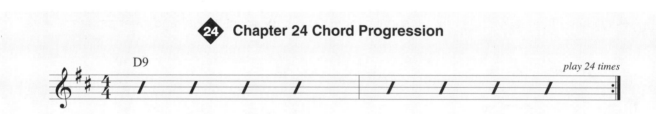

**Chapter 24 Chord Progression**

| Chapter Twenty-Four | **REVIEW** |

1. Be able to construct the Mixolydian scale from any tonic.

2. Know how to use the Mixolydian scale in blues tonality progressions.

3. Be able to play two patterns of the Mixolydian scale from any tonic.

4. Be able to play the given sequences over the entire range of the Mixolydian scale pattern.

5. Be able to play the Mixolydian scale phrases.

6. Be able to improvise over the play-a-long and other progressions furnished in this chapter.

# Mixolydian Phrases

## Objectives

- To present the remaining patterns of the Mixolydian scale.

- To present longer Mixolydian scale phrases.

- To combine the Mixolydian with all other scales and devices over blues tonality progressions.

### EXERCISE 1

This exercise goes through G major scale pattern 4 in diatonic seventh intervals using alternate picking in one position:

## Patterns of the Mixolydian Scale

Here are the remaining patterns of the Mixolydian scale. Again, begin working on these patterns after patterns 2 and 4 are available for immediate recall and use in any key.

**Fig. 1**

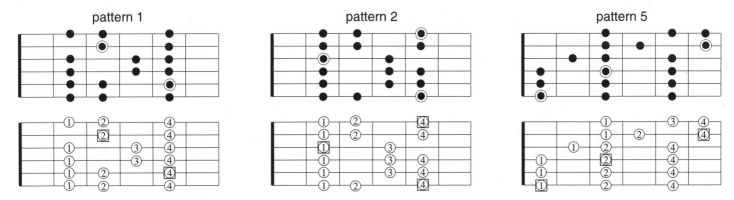

# Mixolydian Scale Phrases

The following phrases are two or four measures in length. Learn to play these ideas while getting a feel for phrases of two and four measures:

**Fig. 2 – Mixolydian phrases**

# Combining All Materials over a Blues Progression

The next exercise combines all devices (scales, arpeggios, call and response, etc.) over a twelve-bar blues progression. There are no bends, hammer-ons, pull-offs, vibrato, slides, or other performance techniques notated. Even the position has been left out. Here is the student's opportunity to apply all of these devices in their own way.

## EXERCISE 2

After reading through the study in a couple of patterns and/or positions, notate your own places to use these devices. Make sure you use each of the devices mentioned.

Now see if you can spontaneously use these devices in different places each time you play the exercise. Soon all of these techniques will become unconscious and will be used wherever you wish to hear them, not just in the blues.

## Chapter 25 Lick

Use this idea over the chapter 25 chord progression. Contrast in your improvised solos is an important element. Too much of any single rhythm, guitaristic device, scale, arpeggio, or even fretboard position can lead to boring and uninteresting solos. It is important to have a large "bag of tricks" of ideas, phrases, rhythms, etc. This idea is essentially a segment that you may want to put into your soloing to contrast the rhythmic density—"a burst of speed." Play this idea mixed in with the other furnished D Mixolydian scale ideas in chapter 25.

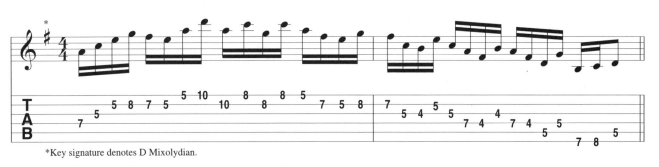

*Key signature denotes D Mixolydian.

## 25 Chapter 25 Chord Progression

This is a D Mixolydian, straight eighth note groove.

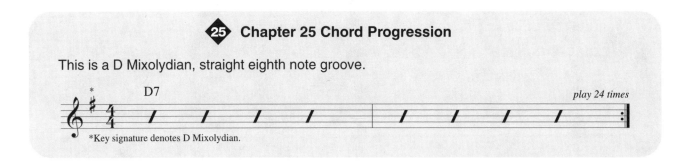

# Summary of the Blues Tonality

As you can see by looking over the last six chapters, the blues tonality is a very unique sound. It combines major and minor tonality scales and progressions. All the items that were introduced under this heading have other uses that will be discussed in upcoming chapters. It is extremely important the student listen to many different artists to learn the nuances and help build a vocabulary of songs and phrases. The influence of the blues can be heard in many different styles of music and is a constantly evolving organism. Listen to as many different artists as possible, incorporating any elements you like into your own style.

| Chapter Twenty-Five | REVIEW |
| --- | --- |

1. When ready, be able to play and use remaining Mixolydian scale patterns in any key.

2. Be able to play the given Mixolydian scale phrases, and make up your own phrases of two and four measures.

3. Be able to interpret the given blues solo using all performance techniques.

4. Be able to combine and use all devices over blues tonality progressions.

# 26 Major Seventh Arpeggios

## Objectives

- To begin a study of the four types of seventh chord arpeggios found in the major and minor scale.

- To understand and be able to construct a major seventh arpeggio.

- To learn how to play the major seventh arpeggio in two octave patterns based on patterns 2 and 4.

- To apply sequences to major seventh arpeggio.

- To combine arpeggio and scalar movement over a major tonality chord progression.

### EXERCISE 1: Stretching Exercise (1 minute)

This warm-up targets the inside of the wrist area, which can become strained (if it is not properly warmed up) from over-exertion. This movement is very simple. Place your right thumb across the inside of your left wrist as if you were going to take your pulse. Then, with a light/easy movement, massage the area in a way that is moving "cross-fiber" at the base of the wrist. You may want to continue the massage up the arm as far as the elbow. Switch hands and repeat the process.

## The Four Seventh Chord Types

When the major and minor scales are harmonized in seventh chords (by adding the note a diatonic third above the fifth of each triad in the harmonized scale) it yields four chord types: major seventh, minor seventh, dominant seventh, and minor seven flat-five (also called a half diminished). Being able to "spell" out these chords using arpeggios gives the improviser the ability to let the listener hear the harmony of a given tune. Arpeggios are also used to give a more interesting contour (shape) to melodic improvisations and lines. We will begin a study of these arpeggios with the major seventh.

## Construction of the Major Seventh Arpeggio

When the major or minor scale is harmonized, it yields two major seventh chords. In the major scale these are the I and IV chords; in the minor scale they are the III and VI chords. It is also important to be able to construct this arpeggio outside of a scale harmony. From any root, the intervals (ascending) are major third, minor third, major third. From a C root this gives these notes:

Be able to construct this arpeggio from any root.

# Patterns of the Major Seventh Arpeggio

Shapes for these arpeggios are based on the five major scale fingering patterns. Here are the five shapes for the major seventh arpeggio:

**Fig. 1**

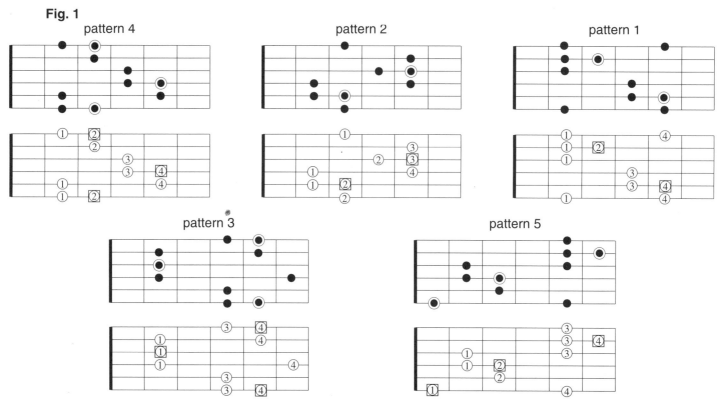

As with the scales, begin by learning patterns 2 and 4, moving on to the remaining patterns only after these two are available for immediate recall and use. Use alternate picking at first, then hammer-ons, pull-offs, and sweep picking.

# Sequencing the Major Seventh Arpeggio

After practicing these arpeggio shapes ascending and descending in order, the notes must be mixed up to create interest. Just like the scale, these arpeggios can be sequenced. Begin by applying each of the following sequences to the full range of the arpeggio shapes in patterns 2 and 4.

**Fig. 2 – Major seventh arpeggio sequences**

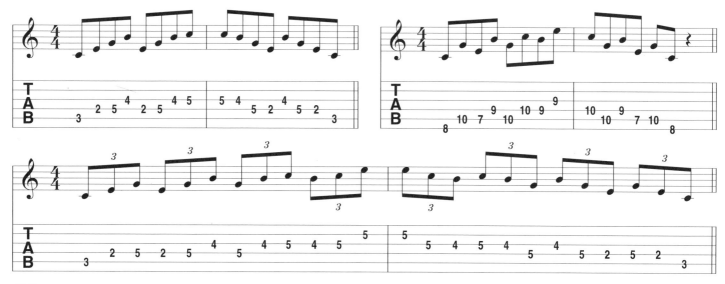

Arpeggios can present some cross-string picking problems, so begin slowly, and for now, use alternate picking.

# Combining Arpeggio and Scalar Movement over a Major Tonality Chord Progression

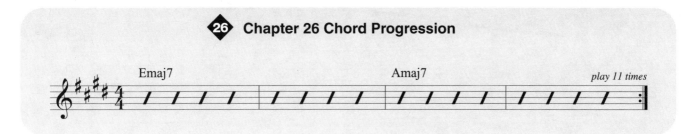

The chapter 26 chord progression is a I–IV progression in the key of E major. Begin playing over this progression with major seventh arpeggios by using pattern 4 for Emaj7 and pattern 2 for Amaj7. Practice switching between the two shapes:

**Fig. 3**

Now, let's use major scale pattern 4 in E and mix it up with the arpeggio tones:

**Fig. 4**

Notice that even through we are using a pattern 2 arpeggio shape for the IV chord, this shape exists within the pattern 4 major scale. Try to view these shapes on their own, as well as part of a scale or key.

## Chapter 26 Lick

Use this idea over the chapter 26 chord progression. It features major seventh arpeggios mixed in with other scale tones.

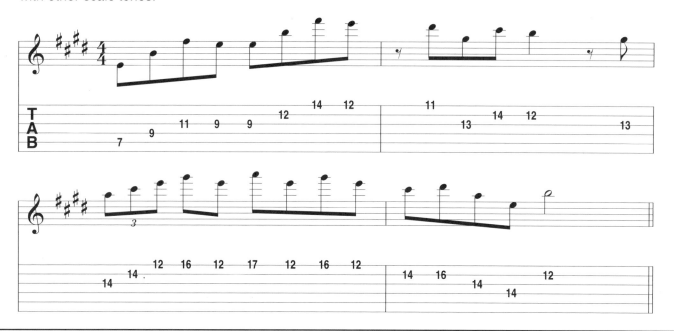

# REVIEW

1. Understand the uses for arpeggios.

2. Be able to construct a major seventh arpeggio from any root.

3. Be able to apply the given sequences to the major seventh arpeggio in patterns 2 and 4.

4. Be able to combine arpeggio and scale motion over the given major tonality chord progression.

# Minor Seventh Arpeggios

## Objectives

- To be able to construct the minor seventh arpeggio from any root.

- To learn two 2-octave patterns of the minor seventh arpeggio.

- To learn sequences and phrases based on the minor seventh arpeggio.

- To combine arpeggio and scale movement over a chord progression and compose your own solo.

**EXERCISE 1**

This is our final diatonic interval leap exercise. It uses the C major scale in diatonic tenth intervals using alternate picking moving up the fretboard on the A and B strings.

# Construction of the Minor Seventh Arpeggio

The minor seventh chord appears as the i, iv, and v in the harmonized minor scale, and as a ii, iii, and vi in the harmonized major scale. From any root the intervals of the arpeggio (ascending) are: minor third, major third, minor third. From a C root this gives these notes:

Be able to construct this arpeggio from any root.

# Patterns of the Minor Seventh Arpeggio

Patterns for this arpeggio are based on the minor scale patterns. Try to see these shapes as parts of a given harmony (ii chord in major harmony or iv chord in minor harmony, etc.) or as the i chord in a minor key. Here are five fingering patterns for the minor seventh arpeggios.

As usual, patterns 2 and 4 are recommended to begin with as they give the player shapes based on the sixth and fifth strings. Learn the remaining shapes when ready, applying all the possible picking combinations. Be able to play two 2-octave shapes from any root.

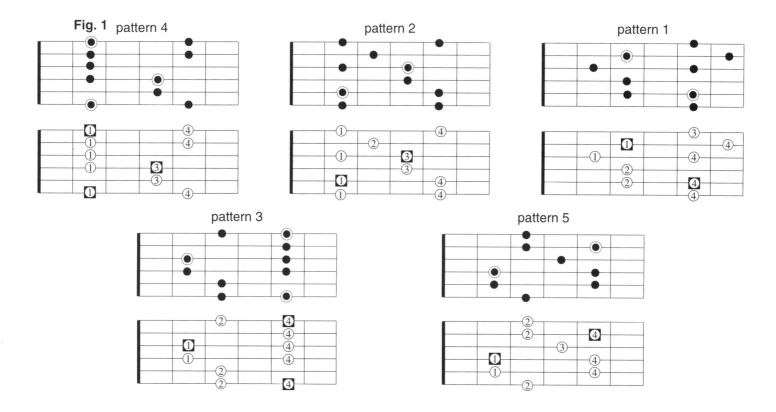

Fig. 1   pattern 4   pattern 2   pattern 1

pattern 3   pattern 5

# Playing Sequences and Phrases Based on the Minor Seventh Arpeggio Shapes

Here are some familiar sequences applied to the minor seventh arpeggio. Be able to play them using alternate picking, then add all possible picking and performance techniques.

**Fig. 2**

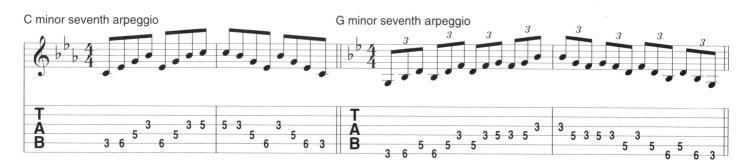

The following figures are phrases based on the minor seventh arpeggio:

**Fig. 3**

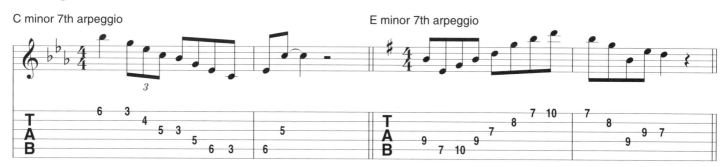

Experiment with these ideas by playing them over chord progressions, and adding or deleting notes.

# Improvising over the Play-a-Long Progression

The chapter 27 chord progression is a i-iv in the key of E minor. The following eight measure study combines arpeggio and scale movement over this progression.

## EXERCISE 2

After learning to play these notes in a pattern of your choice, apply all performance techniques (slides, vibrato, hammer-ons, etc.). After deciding where to place all these elements, notate them on the staff. Spend some time and really figure out where each of these techniques sounds good to you.

### 27 Chapter 27 Chord Progression

This is a straight eighth groove in 4/4, using the i and iv chords in E minor.

## EXERCISE 3

In the space provided, *compose* your own solo using the minor seventh arpeggios and any other melodic devices at your disposal. Notate *all* performance techniques.

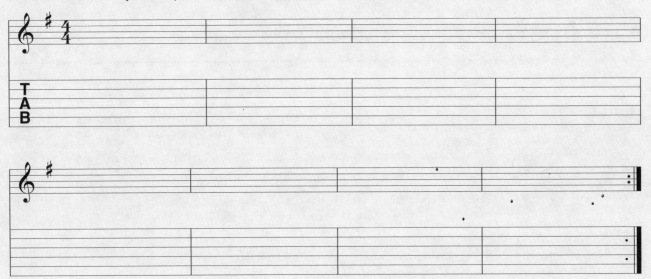

## Chapter 27 Lick

Use this idea over the chapter 27 chord progression. The lick mixes up different shapes of the minor seventh arpeggio as follows:

- Measure 1: E minor seventh arpeggio with the fourth scale degree (borrowed from minor pentatonic).

- Measure 2: Implied B minor seventh arpeggio with the fourth scale degree (borrowed from minor pentatonic).

- Measure 3: Descending A minor seventh arpeggio, descending E minor seventh arpeggio.

- Measure 4: A minor seventh arpeggio with ninth; (also could imply E minor pentatonic).

## Chapter Twenty-Seven          REVIEW

1. Be able to construct the minor seventh arpeggio from any root.

2. Be able to play two 2-octave patterns of the minor seventh arpeggio ascending and descending.

3. Be able to play the given minor seventh arpeggio phrases, and be able to apply the given sequences to the two-octave arpeggio shapes learned.

4. Be able to play the given solo with your own performance techniques.

5. Be able to play the solo which you wrote and notated in the space provided.

# Dominant Seventh Arpeggios

## Objectives

- To be able to construct the dominant seventh arpeggio from any root.
- To learn two 2-octave patterns of the dominant seventh arpeggio.
- To learn sequences and phrases based on the dominant seventh arpeggio.
- To combine arpeggio and scale movement over chord progressions.

### EXERCISE 1: Visualization Exercise

Take a minute before you begin a solo to visualize the contour (structure) of your solo. This is the compositional shape of your solo. For example: you may want to start your solo with a very laid back and sustained feel, then build it up until it peaks at the very last measure of your solo. This is a very common contour.

Other possibilities include:

Peaking in the middle.

Having several points of peak intensity.

Playing at peak levels from start to finish.

Playing with a very sparse, laid back approach.

How to create intensity:

1. Go from a lower pitch range to a higher one.
2. Go from slower to faster rhythms or tempos.
3. Go from "inside" diatonic sounds to subs, and complex and/or non-diatonic sounds.
4. Repetition of an idea or rhythm to build interest.
5. Changes in dynamics (soft to loud, or loud to soft).
6. Change meters (this is usually written into the song).
7. More use of rhythmic syncopation.
8. Wider interval skips.

## Construction of the Dominant Seventh Arpeggio

The dominant seventh chord appears as the V chord in the harmonized major scale, as the VII chord in the harmonized minor scale, and as a I, IV, or V chord in the blues tonality. From any root the intervals of the arpeggio (ascending) are: major third, minor third, minor third. From a C root it gives these notes:

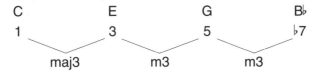

Be able to construct this arpeggio from any root.

# Patterns of the Dominant Seventh Arpeggio

As with previous arpeggio shapes, try to view these as part of a given diatonic harmony (V chord in major, VII chord in minor) and as a I, IV, or V chord in blues tonality. Here are the five fingering patterns for the dominant seventh arpeggio. Begin by learning patterns 2 and 4.

**Fig. 1**

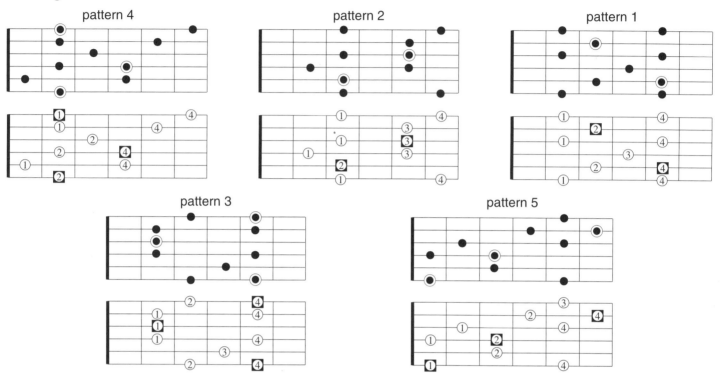

Try to see that these shapes are merely major seventh arpeggios with the seventh lowered. They aren't completely different shapes, just familiar shapes with a variation!

# Playing Sequences and Phrases based on the Dominant Seventh Arpeggio

The following examples use sequences through the arpeggios:

**Fig. 2**

These examples mix up the arpeggio with other notes drawn from the Mixolydian scale with the same tonic.

Be sure to try all kinds of picking possibilities!

# Improvising with the Dominant Seventh Arpeggio

The dominant seventh arpeggio has a very "active" sound. This is due to the presence of a tri-tone interval between the third and seventh. Be aware of this as you begin to use this arpeggio. The following study combines the arpeggio and the Mixolydian scale over the play-a-long progression for chapter 28.

**Fig. 3**

Insert your own performance techniques once the notes have been learned. Try to change these with every play through beforehand, then do it "on the fly."

### 28 Chapter 28 Chord Progression

This is a I dominant seventh to IV dominant seventh groove.

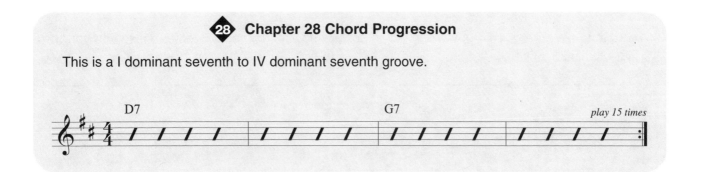

## Chapter 28 Lick

Use this lick over the chapter 28 chord progression. Because the CD track is at a fast tempo, you will need to work up to that tempo gradually. It is recommended that you use hammer-ons and pull-offs to help you execute the lick more easily. Measures 1 and 2 are based on the D7 arpeggio with the notes B, E, and G borrowed from the D Mixolydian scale. Measures 3 and 4 use the G7 arpeggio with the added notes of C, E, and A from the G Mixolydian scale.

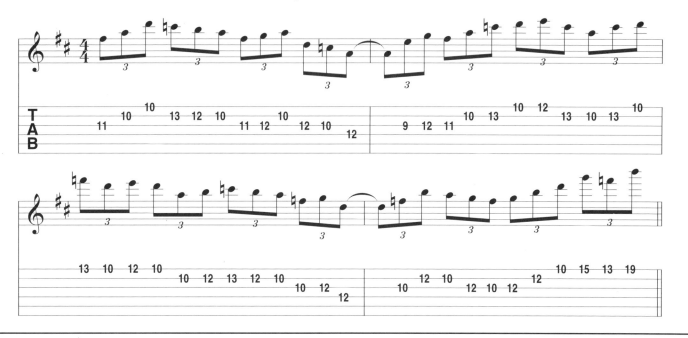

| | | **REVIEW** |
|---|---|---|
| **Chapter Twenty-Eight** | | |

1. Be able to construct the dominant seventh arpeggio from any root.

2. Be able to play two 2-octave patterns of the dominant seventh arpeggio ascending and descending.

3. Be able to play the given study which mixes scalar and arpeggiated movement, inserting your own performance techniques.

# 29 Minor Seven Flat-Five Arpeggios

## Objectives

- To be able to construct the minor seven flat-five arpeggio from any root.
- To learn two 2-octave patterns of the minor seven flat-five arpeggio.
- To learn sequences and phrases based on the minor seven flat-five arpeggio.
- To play the harmonized major and minor scale in seventh chord arpeggios from major scale fingering patterns 4 and 2.
- To use the minor seven flat-five arpeggios over the play-a-long progression.

### EXERCISE 1: Technique Exercise

The following exercise provides you with another way to explore the technique of sweep picking. The idea here is to use a symmetrical chord shape (major 7) and invert it to create a mirror image cascading chord shape (dom13#9, no tonic) that moves up the neck chromatically. The chord shapes are perfect for sweeping because of their one note per string layout. Remember to play each note with a solid attack, cleanly and evenly. Use a metronome! Don't start to lose control or speed up to the point of playing the exercise like a rhythm guitar part! Feel free to take this exercise into the upper reaches of the fretboard, and work your way back down to the original third position Gmaj7 chord.

(cont. up the fretboard)

## Construction of the Minor Seven-Flat Five Arpeggio

The minor seven flat-five arpeggio (also known as the half diminished) appears as the vii chord in the harmonized major scale, and as the ii chord in the harmonized minor scale. Unlike previously learned arpeggios, this sound is very rarely used as a "i" on its own. This is due to its lowered fifth, which forms a tri-tone between the root and fifth, giving it an unstable quality. It is mostly used as a ii chord in minor harmony (part of a minor ii-V-i progression) or as a diatonic substitute for a V chord, though it also has many uses in jazz and fusion styles. Its construction from any root (ascending) is minor third, minor third, (forming a diminished triad) and major third. From a C root this gives these notes:

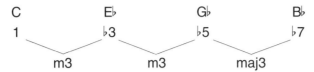

Be able to construct this arpeggio from any root.

# Patterns of the Half Diminished Arpeggio

Patterns for this arpeggio are based on the minor seventh arpeggio shape. Again, we are simply altering one note—the fifth. Try to visualize this arpeggio as a ii chord in minor harmony, or as a substitute for a dominant chord. Begin by learning patterns 2 and 4. Start out by using alternate picking, then apply all possible picking combinations.

**Fig. 1**

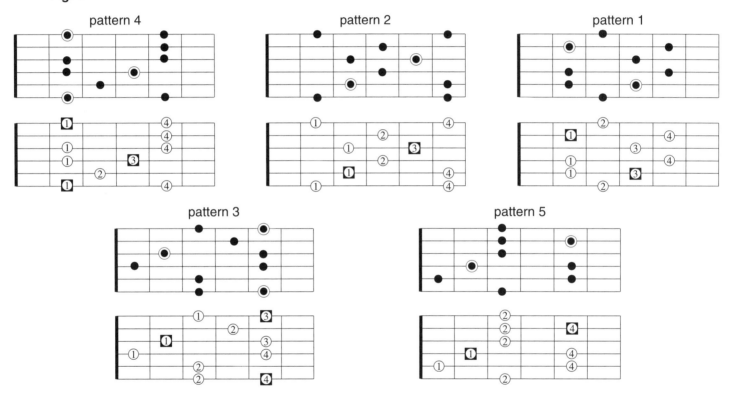

# Playing Sequences and Phrases based on the Minor Seventh Flat-Five Arpeggio

Apply the following sequences to the full range of these arpeggios:

**Fig. 2**

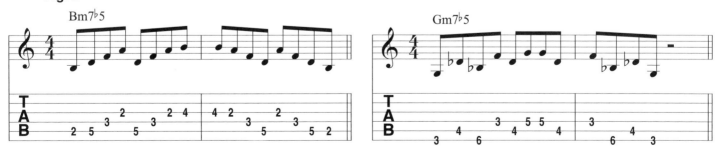

The next phrases add some scale notes to the arpeggio. Note the suggested chord that these are to be played over.

**Fig. 3**

Bm7♭5 arpeggio over G7 chord    C#m7♭5 arpeggio over A7 chord

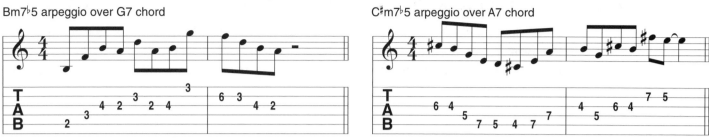

# Playing the Harmonized Major and Minor Scales in Seventh Arpeggios

Learning the half diminished arpeggio has given us all four seventh chord types that appear in the harmonized major and minor scales. The next exercise spells out these arpeggios in one-octave shapes all drawn from pattern 4 of the C major scale:

**EXERCISE 2**

Pieces of these shapes should be familiar, though there are some shapes whose roots aren't on the fifth or sixth string. This allows us to spell out any diatonic chord progression. This next exercise does the same thing in the pattern 2 of C minor scale. Note the different "contour" of how the arpeggios are played:

**EXERCISE 3**

# Using the Minor Seven Flat-Five Arpeggio

The use of the half diminished arpeggio in minor ii-V-i progressions will be covered in upcoming chapters. Let's use this arpeggio as a diatonic substitute for a dominant chord. The following study should be played over the chapter 29 chord progression. It combines the F#m7♭5 arpeggio with the D Mixolydian scale:

**Fig. 4**

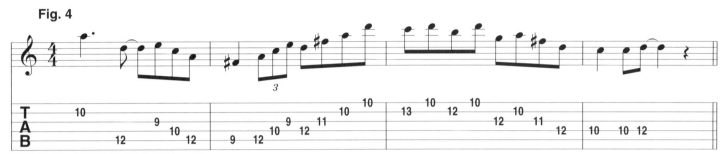

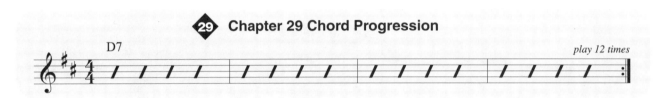

**Chapter 29 Chord Progression**

### Chapter 29 Lick

Use these two ideas over the chapter 29 chord progression. Look for the notes of the F#m7♭5 arpeggio in each example (F#, A, C, E). Apply your own choice of performance techniques; try some "mini-sweep" picking movements on the triplets, and look for places to apply bends and release-bending techniques.

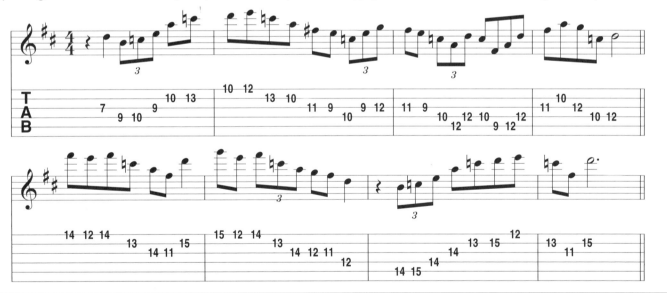

| | **REVIEW** |
|---|---|
| **Chapter Twenty-Nine** | |

1. Be able to construct the minor seven flat-five arpeggio from any root.

2. Be able to play two 2-octave patterns for this arpeggio, ascending and descending.

3. Be able to apply the given sequences to the full range of the arpeggio shapes.

4. Be able to play the harmonized major and minor scales in one-octave seventh chord arpeggios.

5. Be able to use the half-diminished arpeggio over dominant chords.

# 30 Mixing Major Scales and Arpeggios

## Objectives

- To practice combining all the arpeggios in the harmonized major scale using one- and two-octave shapes.

- To practice arpeggiating the ii-V-I chords in major scale harmony.

- To practice mixing scalar and arpeggiated movement over major tonality chord progressions.

**EXERCISE 1: Technique Exercise**

This technique exercise uses wide interval skips to create a finger (and pick) twister!

## Combining and Changing Arpeggios

As stated earlier, arpeggios may be used in two ways: to change the contour (shape) of one's lines, and to spell out the harmony to the listener. When playing over a single chord, the improviser may mix other arpeggios of the key. Which ones? Begin with the diatonic substitutions. The following example should be played over a Dmaj7 chord. It uses the Dmaj7, Bm7, and F#m7 arpeggios:

**Fig. 1**

You can hear that this approach produces some interesting sounds.

Not only can the arpeggio from the root of a chord be played over that chord, the diatonic substitutes may be used as well. As your mastery of harmony and theory grows, you will find many other arpeggios that may be played over any given chord.

# The Major ii-V-I Progression

The ii-V-I progression in major tonality is a very widely used harmonic movement. Many pop songs and jazz tunes use this progression in different ways. It is useful to be able to apply arpeggios to this progression. The following examples uses one-octave arpeggios over a four-measure ii-V-I in the key of C major:

**Fig. 2**

Notice the smooth transition from one arpeggio to the next, as opposed to leaping to the root of each arpeggio. The next example uses two-octave arpeggios and really tries to mix up the notes of these chords:

**Fig. 3**

Now, let's apply some diatonic substitutions:

**Fig. 4**

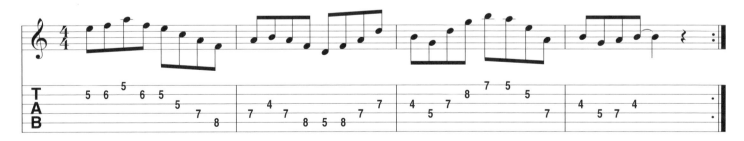

These sounds take time to hear. Keep playing them and creating your own until you can sing these sounds in your head and out loud. Many players develop a vocabulary of ii-V-I ideas.

# Mixing Scalar and Arpeggiated Movement over Major Tonality Progressions

The next example uses a ii-V-I progression in the key of C major and mixes arpeggios (with diatonic substitutions) and major scales (along with major pentatonic scales):

**Fig. 5**

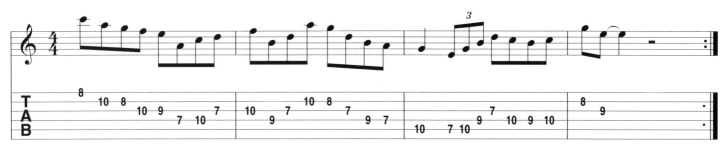

### Exercise 2

In the space provided, compose and write down your own ii-V-I example which mixes up all of these techniques:

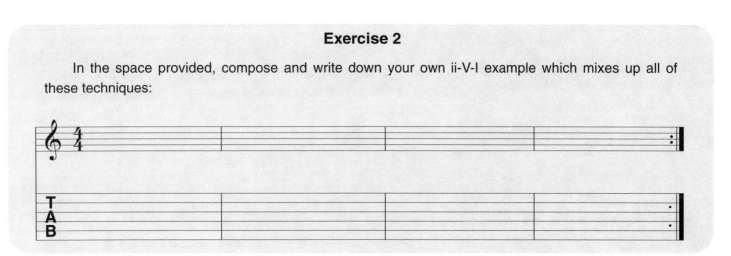

Let's look at the Chapter 30 chord progression (I-IV progression in D major) and lick. The Chapter 30 lick combines the previous elements over this progression.

**Chapter 30 Lick**

**30** **Chapter 30 Chord Progression**

D Major I-IV Latin groove.

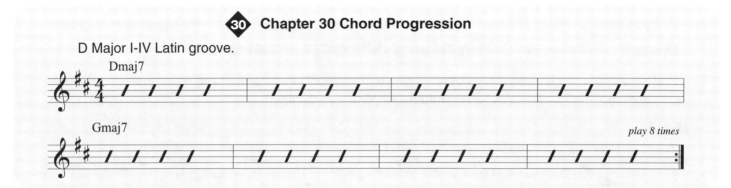

## EXERCISE 3

In the space provided, compose and write down your own example demonstrating these techniques:

---

| **Chapter Thirty** | **REVIEW** |
|---|---|

1. Be able to mix up different arpeggios over major tonality chord progressions (using diatonic substitution arpeggios).

2. Be able to arpeggiate a ii-V-I progression in one- and two-octave shapes.

3. Be able to mix scalar arpeggiated movement over major tonality chord progressions.

4. Be able to play the self-composed examples.

# Mixing Minor Scales and Arpeggios

**31**

## Objectives

- To practice combining the arpeggios in the harmonized minor scale using one-and two-octave shapes.

- To practice arpeggiating the ii, V, and i chords in minor scale harmony.

- To practice mixing scalar and arpeggiated movement over minor tonality chord progressions.

---

**EXERCISE 1: Stretching Exercise (1 minute)**

Take notice of how you are sitting (or standing) as you play the guitar. While this isn't exactly a "stretch," holding your instrument with a relaxed, good posture and body position is essential to your ability to produce music for many years without causing undue stress to your muscles and joints. Check your position right now, are you slumping or hunched over? Is there excess tension in your wrists, hands, neck, or shoulders? Are you able to breathe deeply and feel the flow of blood through your arms? An awareness of these small details can help you to play at your peak.

---

## Combining and Changing Arpeggios

We will continue to combine arpeggios, but in minor tonality. Playing over a single minor chord there are other arpeggios that can be used. This next example is played over an Em7 chord and uses an Em7 and a Gmaj7 arpeggio:

**Fig. 1**

The next example is played over a i-iv progression in E minor and uses a Cmaj7 arpeggio over the iv chord (Am7):

**Fig. 2**

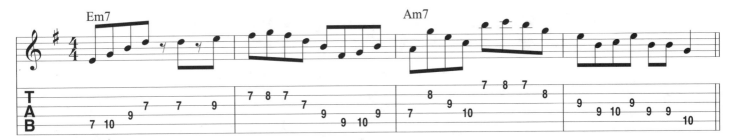

These examples uses a simple diatonic substitution (III for i and VI for iv in minor tonality). Again, as your knowledge of harmony and theory and your "ears" progress, many more possibilities will become available to you. This is just one. Be able to play these examples in two different patterns.

# The Minor II-V-I Progression

The ii-V-i progression in minor tonality is also an extremely popular harmonic movement. The V chord in minor harmony is naturally a minor chord, whereas the overwhelming majority of times the V is made *dominant* in a minor ii-V-i. This alteration of minor tonality yields a new scale which will be covered shortly. All minor ii-V-i progressions will use a dominant V chord.

The next example demonstrates this sound over a four-measure ii-V-i progression in the key of C minor using one-octave arpeggios:

**Fig. 3**

Again, notice the smooth transition between the arpeggios. Using an E♭maj7 arpeggio over the Cm7 chord:

**Fig. 4**

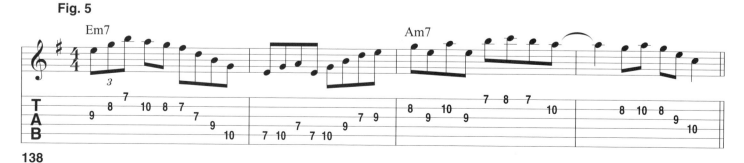

Try these studies out in a different position, as well as different keys. This is not the end-all discussion of minor ii-V-i, it is just a starting point. This progression does have some stylistic leanings, however, its use in many contemporary styles justifies its study. Be able to play these examples in at least two different patterns, adding performance techniques as well.

# Mixing Scalar and Arpeggiated Movement over Minor Tonality Progressions

Let's go back to the i-iv progression in E minor adding scale tones to the arpeggio choices:

**Fig. 5**

## EXERCISE 2

Write your own study using the same tools found in figure 5.

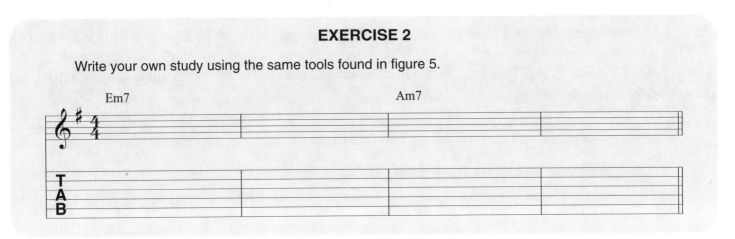

This minor ii-V-i in C minor mixes up scale tones with the arpeggios:

**Fig. 6**

## EXERCISE 3

Write your own ii-V-i study:

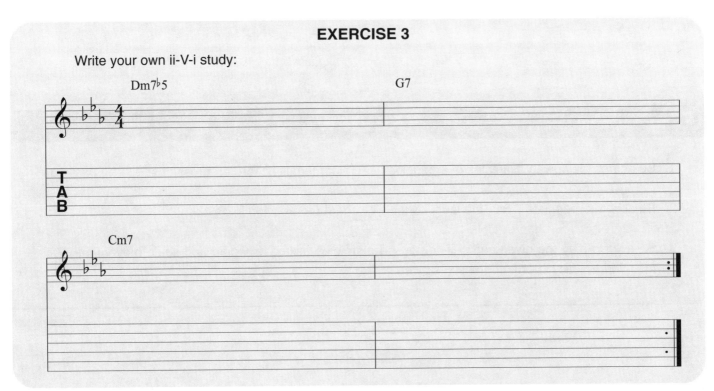

After learning the notes to all of these studies, don't forget to use all performance techniques at your disposal: hammer-ons and pull-offs, slides, bends, vibrato, clean or distorted tone, dynamics, staccato or legato, etc. These techniques add expressiveness and emotion, which are the most important aspects of all music!

**Chapter 31 Lick**

Use this lick over the chapter 31 chord progression.

**31** **Chapter 31 Chord Progression**

G minor ii-V-i groove.

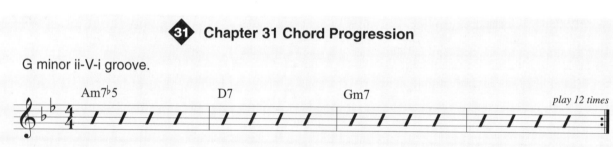

| Chapter Thirty-One | REVIEW |
| --- | --- |

1. Be able to play given examples of arpeggios over minor tonality chord progressions.

2. Be able to arpeggiate a four-measure minor ii-V-i chord progression in any key.

3. Be able to play the given and self-composed examples mixing arpeggio and scale movement over the minor tonality chord progressions given.

# The Harmonic Minor Scale

## Objective

- To learn the construction of the harmonic minor scale, and its application.

- To learn patterns of the harmonic minor scale.

- To learn sequences and phrases based on the harmonic minor scale.

- To apply the harmonic minor scale to minor tonality chord progressions that use a dominant V chord.

### EXERCISE 1: Technique Exercise

This exercise introduces the use of the *sextuplet*. This simply means a quarter note will have six notes of equal value. One obvious benefit of playing the sextuplet rhythm lies in the execution of three note-per-string shapes, which are fairly easy for the guitarist to perform using a hammer-on technique. The technical challenge for some players may lie in the area of accurate timing (make each note equal in value to the next) and "feeling" six notes per beat. Be sure to tap your foot on each quarter note click of the metronome as you play this G major scale. Gradually build your speed.

Use hammer-ons only! Work on precise, even execution, especially when position shifting.

## Construction and Application of the Harmonic Minor Scale

The construction of the harmonic minor scale is based on the natural minor scale. Simply raising the seventh degree of the natural minor scale yields the harmonic minor scale. From a tonic of C, these are the notes:

|   | 1/2 step | | | 1/2 step | | |
|---|---|---|---|---|---|---|
| C | D | E♭ | F | G | A♭ | B | C |
| 1 | 2 | (♭)3 | 4 | 5 | (♭)6 | 7 | 1(8) |

The alteration of this pitch (B♮) makes the V chord of this scale a dominant seventh. When used in minor tonality chord progressions, the dominant V chord lends a greater "push" to resolve to the I chord. Therefore, when a dominant V chord appears in a minor tonality chord progression, the use of the harmonic minor (whose tonic is the same as the key center of the progression) may be used. There are several other specific stylistic usages for the harmonic minor as well.

# Patterns of the Harmonic Minor Scale

The following are the five basic patterns for the harmonic minor scale. Begin by learning patterns 2 and 4, using alternate picking:

**Fig. 1**

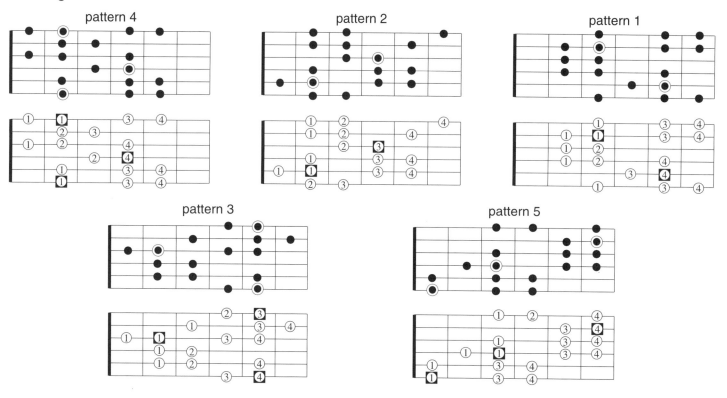

Once you are comfortable with these shapes, apply all picking possibilities (hammer-ons, pull-offs, economy).

# Sequences and Phrases Based on the Harmonic Minor Scale

Take each of the following sequences through the entire range of the fingering patterns for this new scale:

**Fig. 2 – harmonic minor sequences**

The following are phrases that use the harmonic minor scale. Try playing them in different patterns after you have learned them in the positions notated:

**Fig. 3**

# Applying the Harmonic Minor Scale to Minor Tonality Chord Progressions

As stated earlier, the harmonic minor yields a dominant V chord when harmonized. This means that when a dominant V chord appears in a minor tonality chord progression the player may use the harmonic minor scale whose tonic is the same as the key center. In the following progression, use the harmonic minor scale of A in the last measure. For the other chords the natural minor scale should be used:

**Fig. 4**

This next study demonstrates these scale choices. Use all picking possibilities:

**Fig. 5**

As you can hear, the harmonic minor scale really brings out the sound and tendencies of the dominant V chord. The leading tone (in this case G♯) really pushes to resolve to the tonic A.

## EXERCISE 2

In the space provided, write your own study over the chord progression:

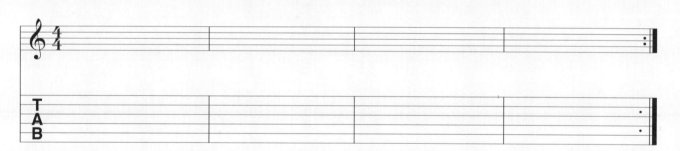

---

### Chapter 32 Lick

Play this over the chapter 32 chord progression.

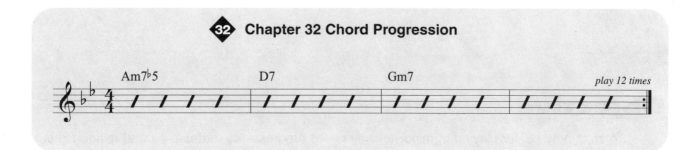

---

**Chapter Thirty-Two**　　　　　　　**REVIEW**

1. Be able to construct the harmonic minor scale from any tonic.

2. Be able to play two patterns (two-octave) for this scale, ascending and descending using alternate picking.

3. Be able to play the given sequences through the full range of two fingering patterns of this scale.

4. Be able to play the given examples of phrases in this scale.

5. Be able to play the given example that uses the harmonic minor scale over a minor tonality chord progression.

6. Be able to play your own example over the given minor progression.

# Minor Key Center Playing

## Objective

- To study key center playing in minor tonality chord progressions that use natural minor, Dorian, and harmonic minor scale harmony.

### EXERCISE 1: Creativity Exercise

Try to further your understanding of the instrument by choosing to solo on any two adjacent strings. You will often see guitarists who seem to be limited to playing solos on the top E and B strings almost exclusively!! You might want to solo on only the D and G strings, or maybe the G and B strings, etc. Try all the combinations. You will find that this will expand your mind and your "fingers"!

## Key Center Playing in Minor Tonality Chord Progressions that Use Seventh Chords

Minor tonality chord progressions are different than major tonality chord progressions in that some of them may mix the harmonies of several different minor scales. (Remember that key center playing involves grouping adjacent chords into a scale and using that scale over all of the chords to produce melodies.) We will be combining harmonies from the natural minor, Dorian, and harmonic minor scales. Let's begin with the following progression:

**Fig. 1**

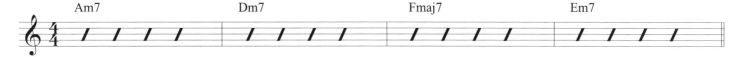

All of its chords are drawn from the natural minor scale. This is a i-iv-VI-V progression in A minor. When the IV chord is a dominant chord or a major triad, the Dorian scale should be used. The natural sixth of the Dorian scale produces a dominant seventh or a major triad. The quality of its IV chord is the deciding factor. Play the following study against the chords noted:

**Fig. 2**

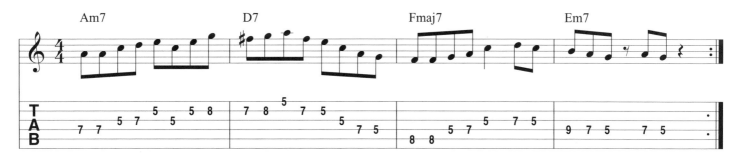

The Dorian scale was used only during the IV chord because the chord following it (Fmaj7) is from the natural minor scale. The next minor scale harmony that we need to adjust our scale choices to is the V dominant chord. When this chord appears, the harmonic minor scale (same tonic as the key center!) should be used. Play:

**Fig. 3**

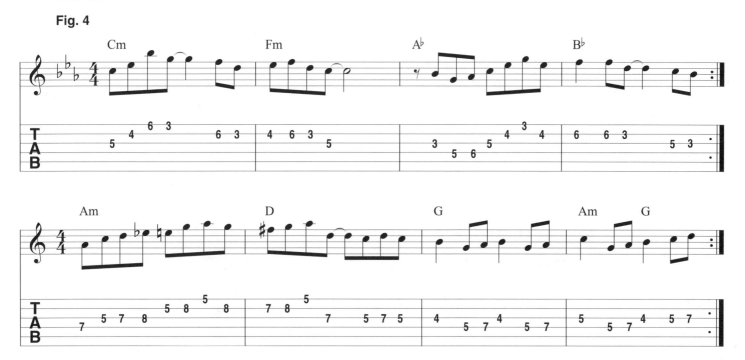

So the progression above will possibly use three different minor scales as the harmony of the progression changes. The most important thing to remember is that a dominant or major triad IV chord uses the Dorian scale, and the dominant V chord uses the harmonic minor scale. (Remember that the tonics of these scales are from the key center!)

# Key Center Playing in Minor Tonality Chord Progressions that Use Triad Harmony

Since the scales are chosen by the major or minor quality and not necessarily the seventh chord type, key center playing over triadic harmony is the same. Watch the quality of the IV and V chord. Play each of the following examples, taking note of which use Dorian, natural, or harmonic minor scale sounds:

**Fig. 4**

## EXERCISE 2

Analyze each of the following progressions, writing down which scales to use. After doing this, record and play over each of them.

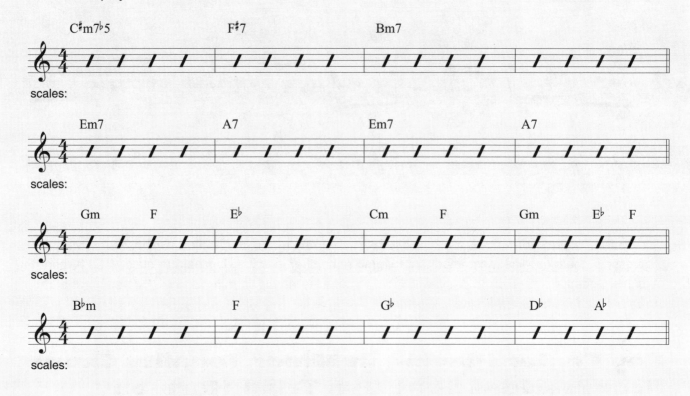

scales:

scales:

scales:

scales:

---

### Chapter 33 Lick

Use this over the chapter 33 chord progression. Analyze it. Which minor scale is the correct choice?

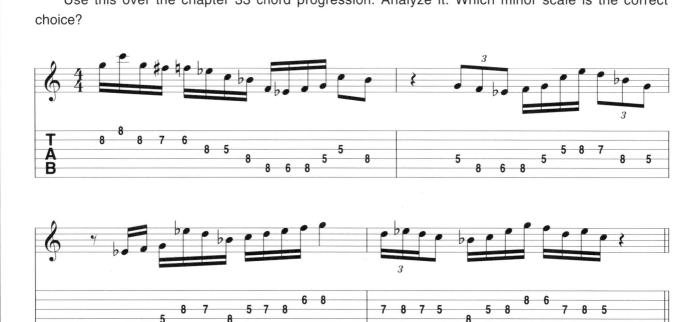

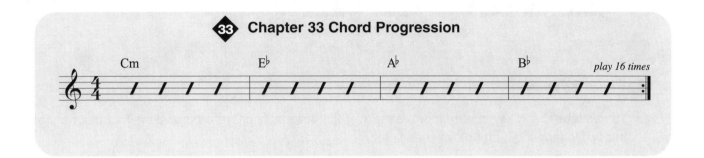

---

| **Chapter Thirty-Three** | **REVIEW** |

1. Be able to analyze minor tonality chord progressions and know when to use natural minor, Dorian, or harmonic minor scales.

2. Be able to play the single line examples and improvise over the given minor tonality chord progressions.

## 34 More Minor Key Center Playing

## Objective

- To continue using key center improvising over minor tonality chord progressions that mix natural minor, Dorian, and harmonic minor scales.

### EXERCISE 1: Technique Exercise

This technique exercise is based on the A major scale, utilizing interval skips of an octave followed by a half step (the ♭9th). There is a very definite quality of chromatic tension going on here. The interesting thing is: the ear will group the steady eighth notes into shifting groups of three notes based on the placement of the chromatic notes (and the octave displacement). Listen for this psycho-acoustic phenomenon as you twist your way through this challenging exercise!

## More Minor Tonality Chord Progressions

Let's continue our study of minor key center playing by looking at the following progressions. Each of them has a specific point to be made.

The next example is a ii-V-i in E minor with a dominant IV chord in the fourth measure:

**Fig. 1**

One way to play over this progression is to use natural minor for the first measure, harmonic minor in the second (due to the dominant V chord) and the Dorian scale for the third and fourth measure (because of the dominant IV chord). Try this:

**Fig. 2**

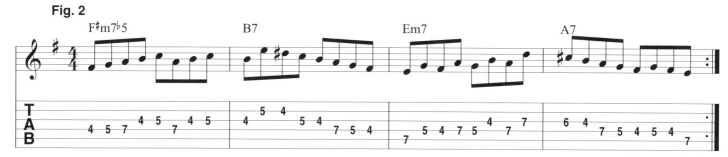

Let's use a few arpeggios, though we are still thinking key of E minor:

**Fig. 3**

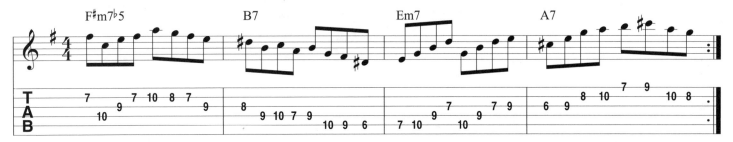

Now take a look at this simpler approach which just uses the minor pentatonic and blues scales:

**Fig. 4**

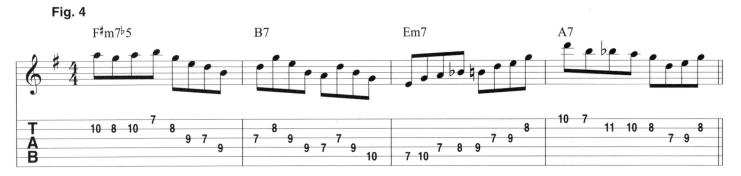

Does that sound good to you? Some people will like it, while others prefer the previous approach. It all depends on the type of sound you wish to convey. The pentatonic and blues scale make it sound "bluesy," whereas the previous approach might sound "jazzier." Here is where style enters the picture. This chord progression could appear in a blues, jazz, or pop context and ultimately the improviser will decide what kind of "flavor" they would like their improvisations to have. Knowing all the tools (scales, arpeggios, etc.) gives the improviser the ability to do this.

Take a look at the following progression:

**Fig. 5**

Is it a progression? It's really a one-chord vamp. The point made here is you could play any minor scale over this vamp. It all depends on the "flavor" you wish your improvisation to have. However, sometimes another instrument is playing notes which will dictate a certain scale and you should be aware of this. If the bass line uses an F, that would be natural minor, if the bass plays an F♯ the Dorian scale. (Also, keyboards or the vocal may use certain notes which will dictate a particular minor scale.) Play each of the following examples over the A minor vamp to get a sense of the kinds of melodies each produces:

**Fig. 6**

**A Dorian**

**A harmonic minor**

Many players (and teachers) treat a single minor chord with the Dorian scale. It is a bright sounding minor scale and it seems to have the most "expected" notes. The natural minor has a very "dark" sound. The harmonic minor has a "Middle Eastern" or "Spanish" sound. Again, try to get a feel for the kinds of melodies each of these scales produces so when faced with a minor chord vamp you can play melodies which produce the effect you want.

Record each of the progressions and improvise over them. Don't forget to use all performance techniques to make your playing musical!

---

### Chapter 34 Lick

Play this over the chapter 34 chord progression.

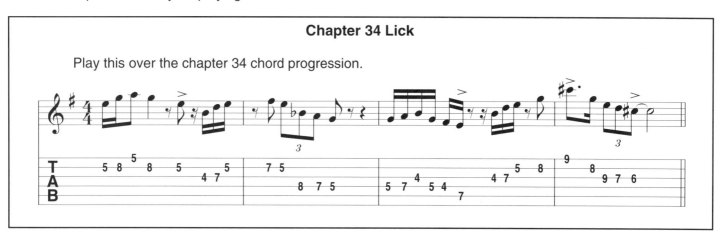

---

### 🔶34 Chapter 34 Chord Progression

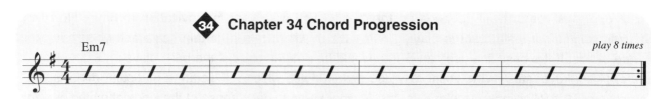

---

| Chapter Thirty-Four | **REVIEW** |
|---|---|

1. Be able to choose the proper scales for minor tonality chord progressions.

2. Be able to make scale choices based on the "flavor" you wish to convey over a minor chord vamp.

3. Be able to improvise over all of the progressions given in this chapter.

# 35 Improvising Over Chord Progressions

## Objective

- To analyze and improvise over three progressions.

### EXERCISE 1: Technique Exercise

This exercise is exclusively about gaining speed, accuracy, and stamina. Go ahead and loop the pattern, playing it non-stop for at least 1 minute. Work your tempos up to 120, 130, 150(!) beats per minute. Alternate pick every note.

# Analyzing and Improvising over Chord Progressions

The three progressions we will be working with mix up chords in major and minor tonality in different keys. Let's take a look at the first example:

**Fig. 1**

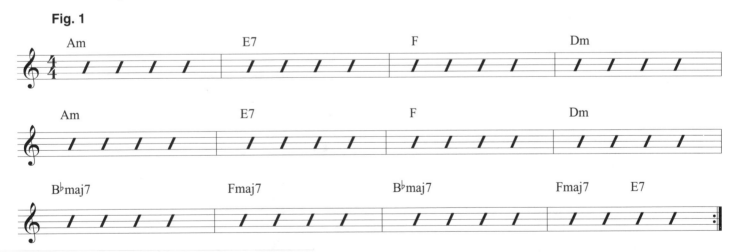

You should be able to figure out what scale to play over the first two lines, whereas the third line introduces a new movement: the idea of a "mini" key center. This is not an official term, it's used to describe a short chord progression that can be more easily seen as a key center on its own. The Bᵇmaj7 and Fmaj7 can be seen as a IV-I progression in the key of Bᵇ major, and the E7 as the V chord of A minor. This progression is in A minor for 8 measures and F major for 3 1/2 measures. Using all devices at your disposal (and you have many!), improvise over the chords.

## EXERCISE 2

When you have become comfortable with the previous chord progression and its scales, write your own study in the space below.

Analyze the next progression, writing down the key centers and scale choices underneath the chords:

**Fig. 2**

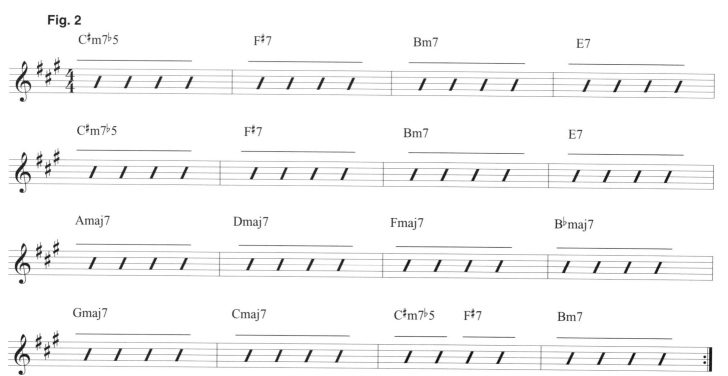

## EXERCISE 3

After improvising over the previous progression for a while, write your own study in the space provided:

Here's another progression to work with. Analyze for key centers and scale choices:

**Fig. 3**

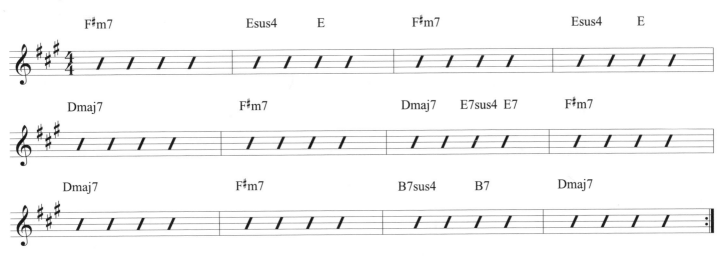

## EXERCISE 4

In the space below, write out a melodic study for the previous chord progression:

Try each of these progressions at different tempos, and with different rhythmic feels! These progressions and lines represent some of the harmonic and melodic concepts presented up to this point that encompass a lot of popular music. Though there is still much to learn, these materials represent a large part of the music you hear everyday. Experiment with writing your own progressions to improvise over. By writing your own solos you will gain a more thorough mastery of the materials presented in this book.

**35** **Chapter 35 Chord Progression**

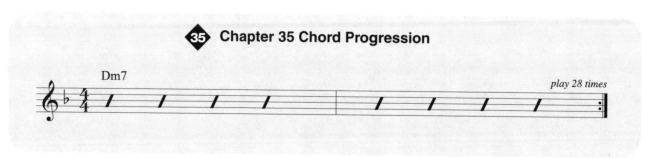

**Chapter 35 Lick**

This minor key etude works well on its own, or try it over a one-chord vamp like the chapter 36 chord progression.

| **Chapter Thirty-Five** | **REVIEW** |
|---|---|

1. Be able to analyze progressions in major, minor, and blues tonality.

2. Be able to choose scales based on your key center analysis.

3. Be able to improvise and play your written studies over these progressions.

# 36 Improvising Over a Song

## Objective

- To improvise over a song.

### EXERCISE 1: Technique Exercise

This exercise works on the ability to place points of emphasis (accents) into your vocabulary by synchronizing strong pick attacks with each consecutive finger of the fretting hand. Let's go back to an "old friend" technique exercise from chapter 1. You may want to create your own variations and combinations; try this with pentatonic scales, or? . . .

(cont. up the fretboard)

## First Steps

The following example is a short yet complete song. It has a four-measure introduction followed by an A section (verse) and a B section (chorus). The first step is to play the song and get familiar with the harmony of each section before we begin improvising.

### The "Feel" and the Tempo

First let's understand the rhythmic interpretation of the piece. The description says "Rock Shuffle." Obviously rock is a stylistic description which would mean using a distorted tone (perhaps), as well as a certain energy level and attitude. Shuffle refers to the rhythmic feel based on the eighth triplet with the first and second triplet being tied.

The metronome setting is very important. It can determine the position you might play a certain unison phrase in, or a fingering or picking strategy for a difficult part. Certain tunes and feels need to be within a certain metronome speed to be effective. Experience and listening are the best teachers here.

### The Intro

This opening four-measure phrase is a unison line with the bass. You must figure out the best place to play it. Set the metronome at the slowest suggested speed and play the Intro. Experiment with open position, then fifth position. Place hammer-ons and pull-offs in different places. (When playing this with a bass player these articulations may have to be worked out together to insure tight phrasing). Test out your positioning at the highest suggested speed.

### The A Section (or Verse)

Now go ahead and play the chords to the A section (verse). Try to hear the key center. What note does the progression seem to revolve around? This approach would be analyzing by "ear." We could also look at the progression and analyze it theoretically. There are three dominant chords in a V-IV-I configuration in E. That would be blues tonality. You could use all your blues tonality scale choices. (Don't forget any individual guidelines they may have!) Don't forget that arpeggios (seventh and triads) are also available to you.

### The B Section (or Chorus)

Play the chords to the B section (chorus). What note do these chords seem to revolve around? It has a minor quality to it. This section is in C♯ minor. Look at the chords. Which minor scales are being used? It looks like the natural minor scale will cover all the chords. Of course the player may use minor pentatonic and blues scales and arpeggios as well.

### Putting it Together

Now we have thought about each of the sections. We have figured out where to play the intro and some scale choices for the A and B sections. Record the song, playing through the form at least four times without stops. (Choose the proper metronome tempo that allows you to do this.) Rewind and play! What do you do? Start with going up and down the scales and mixing up the notes. Then use arpeggios exclusively over each chord. Next time around combine the arpeggios and scales. After that, try mixing in phrases you can recall from earlier chapters (or anywhere else). Try to sing along with your playing. This forces you to phrase in a natural manner as you must breathe.

This song uses only the harmonies presented so far. Although there are many other harmonic devices to learn, what has been learned so far constitutes a large percentage of popular music. Keep on reviewing, and trying to mix all melodic devices with performance techniques. You cannot do this successfully by learning only the techniques of music. The student must listen and constantly expose themselves to new styles, songs, artists, etc. Much can be absorbed by simply listening intently!

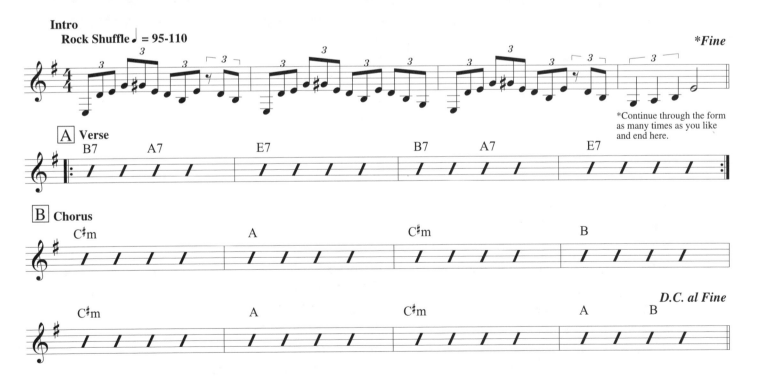

## Chapter 36 Lick

Try this over the chapter 36 chord progression.

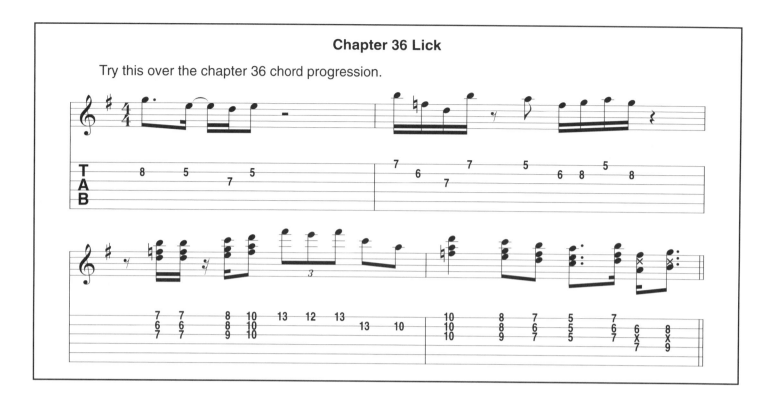

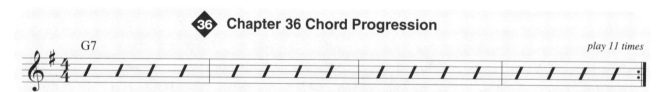

**Chapter 36 Chord Progression**

## Chapter Thirty-Six        **REVIEW**

1. Be able to play the intro riff and the chords to the A and B sections of the song.

2. Be able to improvise over the A and B sections of the song.

# Afterword

The material presented in this book will give the aspiring soloist enough devices to be able to create lines in a majority of the "pop" music heard today. However, there is always more to learn; other scales and harmonic situations need to be mastered if the student wishes to pursue more intense forms of jazz and fusion music.

Rest assured that a careful study of the materials presented will make you a competent and "musical" player. Take your time and be thorough with this book. Always remember to experiment and make these sounds your own.

# The Best in Music Instruction from Hal Leonard

Musicians Institute Press is the official series of Southern California's renowned music school, Musicians Institute. MI instructors, some of the finest musicians in the world, share their vast knowledge and experience for all levels of students in this series of books. For guitar, bass, drums, vocals, and keyboards, MI Press offers the finest music curriculum for higher learning through a variety of series:

- *Essential Concepts* – designed from MI core curriculum programs
- *Master Class* – designed from MI elective courses
- *Private Lessons* – tackle a variety of topics "one-on-one" with MI faculty instructors
- *Workshop Series* – transcribed scores, designed from MI's performance workshop classes

---

## ADVANCED SCALE CONCEPTS & LICKS FOR GUITAR
*by Jean Marc Belkadi*
*Private Lessons*
The complete resource for applying pentatonic, harmonic minor, melodic minor, whole tone, and diminished scales. The CD includes 99 full-band tracks.
_____00695298 Book/CD Pack..................$12.95

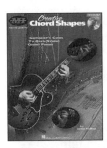

## BASIC BLUES GUITAR
*by Steve Trovato*
*Private Lessons*
Play rhythm guitar in the style of Stevie Ray Vaughan, B.B. King, Chuck Berry, T-Bone Walker, Albert King, Freddie Green, and many more! CD includes 40 full-demo tracks and the instruction covers all styles of blues and the essential chords, patterns and riffs.
_____00695180 Book/CD Pack..................$12.95

## CREATIVE CHORD SHAPES
*Guitarist's Guide to Open-String Chord Forms*
*by Jamie Findlay*
*Private Lessons*
This book/CD pack lets guitarists explore the lush sounds of open-string chords. The CD includes 19 full-demo examples covering: arpeggiated progressions, arpeggiated chords and scalar lines, adding open strings to diatonic chords, and more.
_____00695172 Book/CD Pack....................$7.95

## THE DIMINISHED SCALE FOR GUITAR
*by Jean Marc Belkadi*
*Private Lessons*
Jean Marc Belkadi reveals the secrets of using the diminished scale in over 30 lessons and sample phrases. The CD includes over 30 tracks for demonstration and play-along.
_____00695227 Book/CD Pack....................$9.95

---

## GUITAR BASICS
*Essential Chords, Scales, Rhythms, and Theory*
*by Bruce Buckingham*
*Private Lessons*
This pack gives essential instruction on open chords, barre chords, power chords, strumming; scales, rhythm playing, the blues, and moveable chord shapes. It includes inversions, "color" chords, practice tips, chord charts, songs, and progressions.
_____00695134 Book/CD Pack..................$14.95

## GUITAR HANON
*by Peter Deneff*
*Private Lessons*
51 exercises for the beginning to professional guitarist, covering: diatonic, chromatic, major, minor, dominant, and half-diminished seventh arpeggios, whole tone exercises, diminished arpeggios, and more.
_____00695321..............................................$9.95

## GUITAR SOLOING
*The Contemporary Guide to Improvisation*
*by Daniel Gilbert and Beth Marlis*
*Essential Concepts*
A comprehensive source for mastering the art of single note, melodic improvisation. The CD includes over 30 tracks for demonstration and play-along. The topics covered include: scales, modes, arpeggios, technique and visualization exercises; rock, blues, jazz, and other styles; and sequences, phrases, and licks.
_____00695190 Book/CD Pack..................$17.95

## HARMONICS
*Guitar in the Style of Lenny Breau, Ted Greene, and Ralph Towner*
*by Jamie Findlay*
*Private Lessons*
This pack covers: harp harmonics and natural harmonics; combining harmonics with hammers and pulls; and more. The CD includes 30 full-demo examples.
_____00695169 Book/CD Pack....................$9.95

---

## JAZZ GUITAR CHORD SYSTEM
*by Scott Henderson*
*Private Lessons*
The essential guide to jazz chord voicings and substitutions, complete with a color-coded method for over 500 essential voicings. Players will understand chord functions and their harmonic possibilities better than ever before, as well as inversions, extensions, alterations, and substitutions. Players will also be able to increase their harmonic vocabulary for accompaniment, composing and chord-melody playing.
_____00695291..........................................$6.95

## JAZZ GUITAR IMPROVISATION
*by Sid Jacobs*
*Master Class*
Develop your solo skills with this comprehensive method which includes a CD with 99 full demonstration tracks. Topics include: common jazz phrases; applying scales and arpeggios; guide tones, non-chordal tones, fourths; and more.
_____00695128 Book/CD Pack..................$17.95

## MODERN APPROACH TO JAZZ, ROCK & FUSION GUITAR
*by Jean Marc Belkadi*
*Private Lessons*
Over 30 great lines using a variety of techniques and melodic ideas. Covers: alternate, sweep, and skip picking; major scale, chromaticism, arpeggios, superimposing triads; legato, wide intervals, alterations; and much more. Includes standard notation and tablature.
_____00695143 Book/CD Pack..................$12.95

## MUSIC READING FOR GUITAR
*The Complete Method*
*by David Oakes*
*Essential Concepts*
The ultimate guide to music reading, with over 450 songs and examples. Covers these topics: notes, rhythms, keys, positions, dynamics, syncopation, chord charts, duets, scale forms, phrasing, odd time, and much more!
_____00695192..........................................$16.95

## RHYTHM GUITAR – THE COMPLETE GUIDE

*by Bruce Buckingham & Eric Paschal*
*Essential Concepts*

A comprehensive source for learning rhythm guitar in a variety of musical styles. It covers: open chords, barre chords, and other movable shapes; strumming, finger-style, flatpicking and arpeggiation; common progressions and basic chord theory; triads, sixth, seventh, ninth, and many other chords; and much more.

_____00695188...........................................$16.95

## ROCK LEAD BASICS

*by Nick Nolan and Danny Gill*
*Master Class*

A method exploring the techniques, scales and fundamentals used by the greatest legends of rock guitar. CD includes over 75 full demonstration tracks. Covers pentatonic and diatonic scales, bending, vibrato, lead licks, and more. Includes standard notation and tab.

_____00695144 Book/CD Pack...................$14.95

## ROCK LEAD PERFORMANCE

*by Nick Nolan and Danny Gill*
*Master Class*

Techniques, scales and soloing concepts for guitar complete with a CD containing over 70 full-demo tracks; in-depth study of modes; soloing over chord changes and modulations; harmonic minor, diminished and other scales; blues-based music; and much more!

_____00695278 Book/CD Pack...................$16.95

## ROCK LEAD TECHNIQUES

*by Nick Nolan and Danny Gill*
*Master Class*

Licks, scales, and soloing concepts for guitar, including: picking technique, three-note-per-string scales, sweep picking, fingerpicking, and string skipping, solo constructions, harmonics, and more. CD includes 97 full demo tracks.

_____00695146 Book/CD Pack...................$14.95

---

BASS

## ARPEGGIOS FOR BASS

*by David Keif*
*Private Lessons*

The ultimate reference guide for electric bass! This book covers triad and seventh chord arpeggios, patterns covering the entire 4-string neck, easy-to-use fretboard diagrams, inversions, and more.

_____00695133.........................................$12.95

## BASS FRETBOARD BASICS

*by Paul Farnen*
*Essential Concepts*

All you need to know about the bass fretboard, including: scales, intervals, triads, modal patterns, and fundamentals; keys, fingerings, position playing; arpeggios, turnarounds, walking bass lines; horizontal and vertical playing; for all styles of playing!

_____00695201.........................................$12.95

## BASS PLAYING TECHNIQUES

*by Alexis Sklarevski*
*Essential Concepts*

A comprehensive source for playing bass in a variety of musical styles. Explains: hammer-ons, pull-offs, bends, muting, vibrato; slap bass grooves; essential bass lines and basic theory; exercises, picking suggestions, sample songs; and more!

_____00695207.........................................$14.95

## GROOVES FOR ELECTRIC BASS

*by David Keif*
*Private Lessons*

Grooving – the marriage of the rhythmic feel to the harmony – should be an integral part of a bassist's practice routine, and author David Keif provides a variety of grooves that will help develop any player's skills. This book provides essential patterns and bass lines for rock, pop, blues, funk, R&B, jazz, hip-hop, and other styles. The CD includes 36 tracks for demonstration and play-along.

_____00695265 Book/CD Package.............$12.95

---

## MUSIC READING FOR BASS – THE COMPLETE GUIDE

*by Wendi Hrehovcsik*
*Essential Concepts*

A comprehensive source for sight-reading fundamentals, including notes, rhythms, keys, positions, and scale forms. Also teaches reading from chord symbols, following charts, creating walking bass lines, slides, ghost notes, and other techniques.

_____00695203.........................................$9.95

## ODD METER BASSICS

*A Comprehensive Source for Playing Bass in Odd Time Signatures*
*by Dino Monoxelos*
*Private Lessons*

This pack helps bassists play effortlessly in any time signature! Covers: 3/4, 3/8, 6/4, 6/8, 12/8, 5/4, 5/8, 7/4, 7/8, 9/8, 11/8; multiple-meter charts; playing over the bar line; more! The CD includes 49 full-demo tracks.

_____00695170 Book/CD Pack..................$14.95

---

KEYBOARD

## MUSIC READING FOR KEYBOARD

*by Larry Steelman*
*Essential Concepts*

A complete method for: notes, rhythms, keys, time signatures; treble and bass clefs; right and left hand patterns and accompaniments; popular song styles; repeat signs, accidentals, codas; and more.

_____00695205.........................................$12.95

## R&B SOUL KEYBOARD

*The Complete Method*
*by Henry J. Brewer*
*Private Lessons*

A hands-on guide to the essential R&B soul grooves, chords, and techniques. It covers Gospel and soul keyboard voicings, technique, independence, and the left hand, rhythm, feel, groove, and much more. The CD includes 99 full-band tracks.

_____00695327 Book/CD Pack..................$16.95

## SALSA HANON

*50 Essential Exercises
for Latin Piano
by Peter Deneff
Private Lessons*

50 patterns for the beginning to professional pianist, including the styles of Latin, Cuban, Montuno, Salsa, and Cha-Cha.

_____00695226............................................$10.95

---

### DRUMS

## BRAZILIAN COORDINATION FOR DRUMSET

*Private Lessons
by Maria Martinez*

In this essential method and workbook, Maria Martinez reveals her revolutionary studies for Brazilian drumset coordination. She covers Bossa Nova, Samba and Baiao Ostinatos, 3/4 Bossa Nova/Samba, 7/4 Bossa Nova/Samba, rhythm studies, and more! The CD includes 48 full band tracks.

_____00695284 Book/CD Pack..................$14.95

## CHART READING WORKBOOK FOR DRUMMERS

*by Bobby Gabriele
Private Lessons*

This book/CD covers common symbols and musical shorthand, section figures and ensemble figures, accents, set-up ideas, and embellishment, and swing, big band, and other styles. The CD includes 16 full-demo examples.

_____00695129 Book/CD Pack..................$14.95

## WORKING THE INNER CLOCK FOR DRUMSET

*by Phil Maturano
Private Lessons*

This book/CD pack is a fun, effective, and innovative tool for improving players' chops. The CD includes 16 complete play-along tracks; the lessons cover rock, Motown, funk, shuffle, calypso, big band, fusion, Latin and other grooves; the book includes complete charts with instructional advice and sample groove and fill ideas as well as tips on improving ensemble reading and technique.

_____00695127 Book/CD Pack..................$16.95

---

### VOICE

## SIGHTSINGING

*by Mike Campbell
Essential Concepts*

Includes over 300 examples and exercises and covers: major, minor, modes and the blues; arpeggios, chromaticism, rhythm and counting; professional lead sheets; and much more!

_____00695195.........................................$16.95

---

### ALL INSTRUMENTS

## AN APPROACH TO JAZZ IMPROVISATION

*by Dave Pozzi
Private Lessons*

This book/CD pack explores the styles of Charlie Parker, Clifford Brown, Sonny Rollins, Bud Powell, and others for a comprehensive guide to jazz improvisation. The CD includes 99 tracks for play-along and demonstration. Topics include: scale choices, chord analysis, phrasing, memorization, transposition of solos, melodies, and harmonic progressions, and much more.

_____00695135 Book/CD Pack..................$17.95

## ENCYCLOPEDIA OF READING RHYTHMS

*by Gary Hess
Private Lessons*

A comprehensive guide to: notes, rests, counting, subdividing, time signatures; triplets, ties, dotted notes and rests; cut time, compound time, swing, shuffle; rhythm studies, counting systems, road maps; and more!

_____00695145.........................................$19.95

## GOING PRO

*Developing a
Professional Career
in the Music Industry
by Kenny Kerner
Private Lessons*

Everything you need to know to go pro, including information about personal managers, music attorneys, business managers and booking agents, record companies, A&R, publishing, songwriting, demo tapes and press kits, self-promotion, and much more.

_____00695322.........................................$16.95

---

## HARMONY AND THEORY

*by Keith Wyatt and
Carl Schroeder
Essential Concepts*

This book is a step-by-step guide to MI's well-known Harmony and Theory class. It includes complete lessons and analysis of: intervals, rhythms, scales, chords, key signatures; transposition, chord inversions, key centers; harmonizing the major and minor scales; and more!

_____00695161.........................................$17.95

## LEAD SHEET BIBLE

*by Robin Randall and
Janice Peterson
Private Lessons*

This book/CD package is for the singer, songwriter, or musician who wants to create a lead sheet or chord chart that is easy to follow. The CD includes over 70 demo tracks. The instruction covers: song form, transposition, considering the instrumentation, scales, keys, rhythm, chords, slash notation, and other basics, and more. It also includes sample songs, common terms, and important tips for anyone putting music on paper!

_____00695130 Book/CD Pack..................$19.95

---

### WORKSHOP SERIES

Each of these books includes 10 transcribed scores of music's greatest songs, designed from MI's performance workshop classes. Each part is analyzed to give "behind-the-scenes" understanding of why these songs are classics and how to perform them.

## BLUES WORKSHOP

Help Me • Key to the Highway • T-Bone Shuffle • The Things I Used to Do • and more.

_____00695137.........................................$22.95

## CLASSIC ROCK

Born to Be Wild • Get Back • Iron Man • Sunshine of Your Love • Walk This Way • and more.

_____00695136.........................................$19.95

## R&B WORKSHOP

Ain't No Mountain High Enough • Get Ready • Gimme Some Lovin' • (You Make Me Feel Like) A Natural Woman • Reach Out, I'll Be There • What's Going On • You Keep Me Hangin' On • and more.

_____00695138.........................................$24.95

# Guitar Reference, Instruction & Techniques

## ADVANCED CONCEPTS AND TECHNIQUES

*A Complete Guide To Mastering The Guitar*

The perfect follow-up book for graduates of the Wolf Marshall Guitar Method. With this book, you'll explore the advanced styles of today's greatest players from jazz to monster rock dudes and learn how to combine all you know to make music – your music. Chapters include: triads, scale combining, modes, arpeggios, pentatonics, wide intervals, tap-on technique, and more.

_____00697253.............................$9.95

## ALTERNATE TUNINGS FOR GUITAR

*by Dave Whitehill*

Over 300 tunings from Michael Hedges, Jimmy Page, Sonic Youth, Will Ackerman, Alex de Grassi, Soundgarden, Joni Mitchell, and many more. Includes drop, open, modal, unison, slack, and hybrid tunings.

_____00695217.............................$4.95

## BASIC GUITAR ADJUSTMENTS & SETUPS

*by John Boehnlein*

An essential guide to guitar maintenance, covering: essential tools and inspection tips; neck, action, intonation, and pickup adjustments; re-stringing; adjusting vibrato bridges; and more.

_____00695149.............................$4.95

## BLUES YOU CAN USE

*by John Ganapes*

A comprehensive source for learning blues guitar, designed to develop both your lead and rhythm playing. Covers all styles of blues, including Texas, Delta, R&B, early rock and roll, gospel, blues/rock and more. Includes 21 complete solos; blues chords, progressions and riffs; turnarounds; moveable scales and soloing techniques; string bending; audio with leads and full band backing; and more!

_____00695007 Book/CD Pack..................$19.95
_____00695276 Spanish Edition ................$19.95

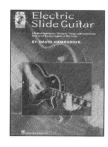

## ELECTRIC SLIDE GUITAR METHOD

*by David Hamburger*

This book/CD pack is a comprehensive examination of slide guitar fundamentals. You get lessons on the styles of Duane Allman, Dave Hole, Ry Cooder, Bonnie Raitt, Muddy Waters, Johnny Winter, and Elmore James. Also includes: sample licks and solos; info on selecting a slide and proper setup; backup/rhythm slide playing; standard and open tunings; and more.

_____00695022 Book/CD Pack...................$19.95

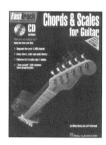

## FASTTRACK GUITAR CHORDS & SCALES

Over 1,400 chords, essential scale and mode patterns, including pentatonic, diatonic, harmonic minor, melodic minor, and many other scales. PLUS! Unique play-along "jam session" with 20 different chord progressions.

_____00697291 Book/CD Pack...................$9.95

## THE GUITAR F/X COOKBOOK

*by Chris Amelar*

The ultimate source for guitar tricks, effects, and other unorthodox techniques. This book demonstrates and explains 45 incredible guitar sounds using common stomp boxes and a few unique techniques, including: pick scraping, police siren, ghost slide, church bell, jaw harp, delay swells, looping, monkey's scream, cat's meow, race car, pickup tapping, and much more.

_____00695080 Book/CD Pack...................$14.95

## GUITAR LICKS

*by Chris Amelar*

Learn great licks in the style of players like Clapton, Hendrix, Hammett, Page and more. Includes two complete solos; 40 must-know licks for rock and blues; info on essential techniques; standard notation & tab; and more. CD features demos of every technique, lick and solo in the book.

_____00695141 Book/CD Pack..................$14.95

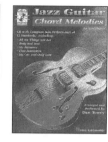

## JAZZ GUITAR CHORD MELODIES

*arranged & performed by Dan Towey*

This book/CD pack includes complete solo performances of 12 standards, including: All the Things You Are • Body and Soul • My Romance • How Insensitive • My One and Only Love • and more. The arrangements are performance level and range in difficulty from intermediate to advanced.

_____00698988 Book/CD Pack..................$19.95

## TERRIFYING TECHNIQUE FOR GUITAR

*by Carl Culpepper*

The ultimate source for building chops while improving your technical facility and overcoming physical barriers. Covers: alternate, economy, hybrid, and sweep picking; symetrical, chromatic, and scale exercises; arpeggios, tapping, legato, and bending sequences – over 200 exercises in all. CD includes full demonstrations of the exercises.

_____00695034 Book/CD Pack..................$14.95

## ULTIMATE EAR TRAINING FOR GUITAR AND BASS

*by Gary Willis*

Everything you need to improve your ear training, including a CD with 99 full-demo tracks, vital information on intervals, rhythms, melodic shapes, inversions, scales, chords, extensions, alterations, fretboard visualization, and fingering diagrams.

_____00695182 Book/CD Pack.................$12.95

## THE WOODSHEDDING SOURCE BOOK – THE ULTIMATE PRACTICE MANUAL

*by Emile De Cosmo*

This book presents a proven approach to practicing and is, in essence, woodshedding in book form. Rehearsing with this method daily will improve your technique, reading ability, rhythmic and harmonic vocabulary, eye/finger coordination, endurance, range, theoretical knowledge, and listening skills – all which lead to superior improvisational skills. The CD provides full rhythm section and harmonic background for all 66 exercises.

_____00842000 Book/CD Pack..................$19.95

# Bass Reference, Instruction & Techniques

## BASS IMPROVISATION

*The Complete Guide to Soloing*
*by Ed Friedland*
This book/CD pack is designed to help players master the art of improvisation. The CD includes over 50 tracks for demonstration and play-along. The book works with electric or acoustic bass and covers: modes, harmonic minor, melodic minor, blues, pentatonics, diminished, whole tone, Lydian b7, Mixolydian b13, and other important scales; phrasing, chord scale concepts, melodic development, guide tones, and resolutions; plus how to use your ear, practice tunes, and much more!

_____00695164 Book/CD Pack.................$17.95

## FUNK BASS

*by Jon Liebman*
Critically acclaimed as the best single source for the techniques used to play funk and slap-style bass! Includes a foreword by John Patitucci and is endorsed by Rich Appleman of the Berklee College Of Music, Will Lee, Mark Egan, Stuart Hamm and many others! Features several photos and a special section on equipment and effects. A book for everyone – from beginners to advanced players! Includes a 58-minute audio accompaniment.

_____00699347 Book/Cassette Pack..........$14.95
_____00699348 Book/CD Pack.................$17.95

## FUNK/ FUSION BASS

*by Jon Liebman*
This follow-up to Funk Bass studies the techniques and grooves of today's top funk/fusion bass players. It includes sections on mastering the two-finger technique, string crossing, style elements, establishing a groove, building a funk/fusion soloing vocabulary, and a CD with over 90 tracks to jam along with. Features a foreword written by Earth, Wind And Fire bassist Verdine White.

_____00696553 Book/CD Pack.................$19.95

## FINGERBOARD HARMONY FOR BASS

*A Linear Approach For 4-, 5- and 6-String Bass*
*by Gary Willis*
A comprehensive source for learning the theory and geometry of the bass fingerboard by one of today's leading players and instructors. Audio features Gary Willis demonstrating 99 examples and exercises.

_____00695043 Book/CD Pack.................$17.95

---

## JAZZ BASS

*by Ed Friedland*
This book/CD pack features over 50 examples covering walking bass, the two feel, 3/4 time, Latin, and ballads. It covers soloing, performance protocol, and includes seven complete tunes.

_____00695084 Book/CD Pack.................$17.95

## JUMP 'N' BLUES BASS

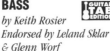

*by Keith Rosier*
Essential jump/swing and modern blues bass lines for electric and upright players. Includes lessons and music in the style of Willie Dixon, Larry Taylor, Edgar Willis, Duck Dunn, Tommy Shannon, and more! The CD includes a lives blues band with over 20 play-along tracks.

_____00695292 Book/CD Pack.................$14.95

## LOST ART OF COUNTRY BASS

*by Keith Rosier*
*Endorsed by Leland Sklar & Glenn Worf*
An introduction to country bass for electric or upright players. This book/CD pack is an insider's look at country bass playing on stage and in the studio. The book includes lessons and music in the style of Hank Williams, Lefty Frizzel, Marty Stuart, David Ball, and more. The CD includes 35 songs with full band backing. You'll learn classic and modern country bass lines, how to be a studio bassist, how to read music with the Nashville Number System, and more!

*"A killer country primer."*
*– Bass Player magazine*
_____00695107 Book/CD Pack.................$17.95

## MUTED GROOVES

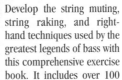

*by Josquin des Pres*
Develop the string muting, string raking, and right-hand techniques used by the greatest legends of bass with this comprehensive exercise book. It includes over 100 practical exercises with audio accompaniments for each.

_____00696555 Book/CD Pack.................$16.95

---

## REGGAE BASS

*by Ed Friedland*
The complete guide to reggae and Jamaican bass styles, covering early ska, rock steady, roots reggae, dub, modern ska, dance hall, and more. The book includes performance tips and lessons, authentic grooves and riddims, and more. The CD includes 47 full-demo tracks.

_____00695163 Book/CD Pack.................$12.95

## ROCK BASS

*by Jon Liebman*
Learn the essential rock grooves and bass lines in the style of Paul McCartney, John Entwistle, John Paul Jones, Geddy Lee, Sting, Billy Sheehan, Flea, and many more! The CD includes 99 full-demo tracks for every exercise in the book and the book itself includes tips on all the essential techniques, grooves and bass lines from the 1950s through the 1990s. Also includes tips on equipment, effects, and listening suggestions.

_____00695083 Book/CD Pack.................$17.95

## RON CARTER – BUILDING JAZZ BASS LINES

Ron Carter is a living legend, having been an integral part of the Miles Davis group and V.S.O.P. In this book/CD package, Ron shows the student how to create more creative bass lines in a step-by-step process that will yield creative results in a very short time. The exercises in the book (blues in major and minor keys, 3/4 blues), as well as three of Ron's compositions, are performed by an all-star rhythm section of Ron on bass, Mulgrew Miller on piano, Ofer Ganor on guitar, and Lewis Nash on drums. Ron's part can be isolated on each track, so you can listen to him play the exercises, play along with him, and then turn his track off and create your own bass lines with the guitar, piano, and drums.

_____00841240 Book/CD Pack.................$19.95

## 6-STRING BASSICS

*by David Gross*
The complete guide for mastering the six-string bass. This book/CD pack covers scales, arpeggios, modes, chord forms, two-handed tapping, alternative techniques, chromatic exercises and theory concepts. The CD includes 99 full-demo tracks.

_____00695221 Book/CD Pack.................$12.95

# Keyboard Reference, Instruction & Techniques

### ASPIRING JAZZ PIANIST
*by Debbie Denke*
There is no joy like that of expressing yourself through musical improvisation. This book/CD pack will show you how to arrange and improvise to popular and jazz tunes in your own style, using a clear, step-by-step method developed over many years by successful jazz pianist and teacher Debbie Denke. It can be used for personal instruction or as a classroom text. The CD features both solo piano demonstrations and bass and drum accompaniments that let you practice playing with a rhythm section.
_____00290480 Book/CD Pack....................$24.95

### BLUES RIFFS FOR PIANO
*by Ed Baker*
*Great Riffs Series*
*Cherry Lane Music*
The definitive source for blues riffs and licks! Features performance notes for and accompanying audio examples of fills and embellishments, turnarounds, tags and licks in the style of Ray Charles, Dr. John, Professor Longhair, and Johnny Johnson.
_____02503615 Book/CD Pack...................$17.95

### COUNTRY RIFFS FOR PIANO
*by George Wurzbach*
*Great Riffs Series*
*Cherry Lane Music*
The ultimate source for learning country riffs and licks! Features concise performance notes on how to play more than 25 fills, turnarounds, tags, comping patterns, and solos. Also includes a history of the piano in country music, as well as an accompanying audio cassette or CD of the examples, all in one riff-packed, easy-to-follow book.
_____02503613 Book/CD Pack...................$17.95

### DR. JOHN TEACHES NEW ORLEANS PIANO VOLUME 1 – IN-DEPTH SESSIONS WITH A MASTER MUSICIAN
*Homespun Listen & Learn Series*
Mac "Dr. John" Rebennack, a veritable encyclopedia of music and lore, immerses you in all aspects of New Orleans boogie and blues piano. This intimate session with the legendary "Night Tripper" will help you build a solid repertoire and acquire a wealth of essential licks, runs, turnarounds, rhythms and techniques. Even non-players will love this guided tour of a great American tradition.
_____00699090 Book/CD Pack...................$19.95

### EXPLORING BASIC BLUES FOR KEYBOARD
*by Bill Boyd*
This book introduces a blues scale system that produces idiomatic sounds characteristic of early blues, dixieland, boogie, swing and rock. Instruction begins with one-measure phrases followed by a step-by-step approach to twelve-measure improvisation.
_____00221029............................................$12.95

### EXPLORING JAZZ SCALES FOR KEYBOARD
*by Bill Boyd*
Scales provide the basis for jazz improvisation and fill-ins. The scales presented in this book produce idiomatic sounds associated with many jazz styles. Boyd explores the jazz scales and examines their potential, giving the player more improvisation resources. Each chapter includes charts with the scales written in all keys with suggested fingerings and a list of chords which complement each scale. Music examples apply the scales to jazz chord progressions and compositions. Upon completion, the student will gain new insights into the practical application of jazz scales and will be able to enhance performance.
_____00221015............................................$12.95

### JAZZ PIANO – CONCEPTS & TECHNIQUES
*by John Valerio*
This book provides a step-by-step approach to learning basic piano realizations of jazz and pop tunes from lead sheets. Systems for voicing chords are presented from the most elementary to the advanced, along with methods for practicing each system. Both the non-jazz and the advanced jazz player will benefit from the focus on chords, chord voicings, harmony, melody and accompaniment, and styles.
_____00290490...........................................$16.95

### JAZZ RIFFS FOR PIANO
*by Frank Feldman*
*Great Riffs Series*
*Cherry Lane Music*
Learn the hottest tags, patterns, turnarounds, and solos in the style of the jazz world's legendary talents, such as Bud Powell, Thelonious Monk, George Shearing, Red Garland, Erroll Garner, Chick Corea, Bill Evans, and Keith Jarrett. Included in this book/audio package are detailed performance notes for all examples.
_____02503620 Book/CD Pack..................$17.95

### THE POP PIANO BOOK
*by Mark Harrison*
A complete ground-up method for playing contemporary styles spontaneously on the keyboard. This 500-page book includes review of harmonic and rhythmic concepts, application of harmony to the keyboard in all keys, and then specific instruction for playing in pop, rock, funk, country, ballad, new age, and gospel styles. This unique book is endorsed by Grammy-winners and top educators. 498 pages
_____00220011............................................$39.95

### THE SOURCE
*by Steve Barta*
Solid information regarding scales, chords, and how these two work together. The Source provides clear and complete right and left hand piano fingerings for scales, chords, and complete inversions. With over twenty different scales, each written in all twelve keys, The Source is the most complete collection of contemporary and traditional scales ever compiled into one book.
_____00240885............................................$12.95

### THE ULTIMATE KEYBOARD CHORD BOOK
*The Ultimate Keyboard Chord Book* is a comprehensive volume containing over 1600 chord diagrams with 77 different chords for each key. Includes treble and bass clef notation for all chords in the book as well as a chord symbol chart. An introductory section explains the theory of chord construction.
_____00290045............................................$12.95

### VOICINGS FOR JAZZ KEYBOARD
*by Frank Mantooth*
A respected soloist, clinician and writer, Mantooth has written this book for any keyboard player interested in developing better jazz chord voicing. Written more as a "how-to" book than a textbook, Voicings will make a valuable addition to the library of any performer, arranger, teacher or jazz theorist.
_____00855475............................................$12.95

# Drum Reference, Instruction & Techniques

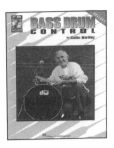

### BASS DRUM CONTROL

*by Colin Bailey*
This perennial favorite among drummers helps players develop their bass drum technique and increase their flexibility through the mastery of exercises. Now available with CD.
_____06620020 Book/CD Pack..................$17.95

### THE COMPLETE DRUMSET RUDIMENTS
*by Peter Magadini*
Use your imagination to incorporate these rudimental etudes into new patterns that you can apply to the drumset or tom toms as you develop your hand technique with the Snare Drum Rudiments, your hand and foot technique with the Drumset Rudiments and your polyrhythmic technique with the Polyrhythm Rudiments. The recording includes demonstrations of the rudiments and four drum solos utilizing all of the rudiments.
_____06620016 Book/CD Pack..................$14.95

### CREATIVE TIMEKEEPING FOR THE CONTEMPORARY JAZZ DRUMMER
*Rick Mattingly*
Combining a variety of jazz ride cymbal patterns with coordination and reading exercises, *Creative Timekeeping* develops true independence: the ability to play any rhythm on the ride cymbal while playing any rhythm on the snare and bass drums. It provides a variety of jazz ride cymbal patterns as well as coordination and reading exercises that can be played along with them. Five chapters: Ride Cymbal Patterns; Coordination Patterns and Reading; Combination Patterns and Reading; Applications; and Cymbal Reading.
_____06621764..............................$8.95

### THE DRUM PERSPECTIVE

*by Peter Erskine*
*edited by Rick Mattingly*
*The Drum Perspective* is like a series of private lessons that can be enjoyed anywhere, at any time. It is not written for drummers only, however! It is also designed for other instrumentalists and vocalists who work with drummers, bandleaders, educators and students of music, and anyone curious about the art of rhythm. This pack also includes a CD compilation of tracks that represent some of Erskine's best work, including: But Is It Art? • L.A. Stomp • Straphangin' • and more. Also includes transcriptions and charts of many of the CD performances, plus specific exercises designed to enhance a drummer's ability, creativity, and awareness.
_____06620015 Book/CD Pack ...............$19.95

### THE DRUMMER'S ALMANAC
*by Jon Cohan*
This celebration of the art of drumming is a must-have for all drummers, beginning to advanced. With essential tips on techniques and tongue-in-cheek anecdotes, *The Drummer's Almanac* is very informative and very fun. Includes lots of photographs, interviews, quotes, jokes, helpful hints, and more. Chapters include: A Short History of the Drum Set; A Natural Approach to Drumming by Dave Weckl; Care and Maintenance of Your Drums; A Day in the Life of Anton Fig; Some Handy Grooves; Drum Miking Basics; and much more!
_____00330237.............................$12.95

### THE DRUMSET MUSICIAN

*by Rod Morgenstein and Rick Mattingly*
This beginning- to intermediate-level book contains hundreds of practical, usable beats and fills. It teaches how to apply a variety of patterns and grooves to the actual performance of songs. The CD includes demos and 14 play-along tracks covering rock, blues and pop styles, with detailed instructions on how to create exciting, solid drum parts. It's the most realistic – and fun! – way to learn drums.
_____06620011 Book/CD Pack..................$19.95

### INNER RHYTHMS – MODERN STUDIES FOR SNARE DRUM
*by Frank Colonnato*
*Inner Rhythms* presents interesting and challenging etudes for snare drum based on the rhythms of contemporary music, including a variety of time signatures, shifting meters and a full range of dynamics. These studies will help improve reading skills as well as snare drum technique, and will provide insight to the rhythmic demands of modern music.
_____06620017.............................$7.95

### JOE MORELLO – MASTER STUDIES
*Modern Drummer Books*
This is "the" book on hand development and drumstick control. *Master Studies* focuses on these important aspects: accent studies, buzz-roll exercises, single and double-stroke patterns, control studies, flam patterns, dynamic development, endurance studies, and much more!
_____06631474.............................$9.95

### LEARN TO PLAY THE DRUMSET

*by Peter Magadini*
This method has been written to teach the basics of the drum set in the shortest amount of time. The method is unique in that it is a beginning course that starts the student out on the entire drum set.
_____06620000  Book One..........................$5.95
_____06620002  Book One/Cassette Pak.....$12.95
_____06620001  Book Two..........................$5.95
_____06620005  Book Two/Cassette Pak.....$12.95
_____06620050  Spanish Edition .................$4.95

### METHOD BOOK 1
*by Blake Neely &*
*Rick Mattingly*
In this beginner's guide to drums, you'll learn music notation, riffs and licks, syncopation, rock, blues and funk styles, and improvisation. Includes over 75 songs and examples.
_____00697285 Book/CD Pack....................$7.95

### MODERN PERCUSSION GROOVES

*by Glen Caruba*
*Centerstream Publishing*
Glen Caruba's first book, Afro-Cuban Drumming, touched on basic Latin percussion styles. This follow-up teaches how to incorporate these traditional rhythms and techniques into modern pop and rock playing. Covers instrument playing tips (congas, bongo, timbale, cowbell, shakers and more), funk grooves, pop ballads, Afro-Cuban 6/8, jazz-fusion grooves, cha-cha pop, and lots more. The CD features 40 tracks of examples.
_____00000228 Book/CD Pack..................$16.95

### NEW DIRECTIONS AROUND THE DRUMS
*by Mark Hamon*
*Centerstream Publications*
Endorsed by noteables like Hal Blain, Peter Erskine, Jim Chapin, and more, this book features a comprehensive, non-rudimental approach to the drumset for beginners to professionals! It combines straight drum-to-drum patterns with cross-sticking configurations, and includes open-ended free-style drum patterns for use as solos and fills.
_____00000170.........................$14.95

# Vocal Publications

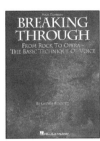

### BREAKING THROUGH

*From Rock To Opera – The Basic Technique Of Voice*
by Gloria Bennett
Author and voice teacher Gloria Bennett has taught Axl Rose of Guns N'Roses, Dexter of Offspring, and Anthony Kiedis of the Red Hot Chili Peppers, and others. Her comprehensive and practical book offers a clear explanation of the voice as an instrument, and proper vocal technique. Through examples, anecdotes, and exercises, *Breaking Through* provides for both the novice and professional vocalist a vital sourcebook for maintaining and enhancing the quality of the voice. 8-1/2" x 11"

_____ 00330258 ........................................$14.95

### LEARN TO SING HARMONY

*taught by Cathy Fink, Marcy Marxer, Robin and Linda Williams*
*Homespun*
Four wonderful singers teach beginners or experienced singers the principles of two-, three-, and four-part harmonies to enhance favorite folk, country, and bluegrass songs. A special feature: the parts are recorded on separate stereo tracks for practicing with either the melody or the harmony line. Teaches 20 songs.

_____ 00641424 Book/3-CD Pack...............$34.95

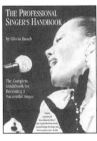

### THE PROFESSIONAL SINGER'S HANDBOOK

*by Gloria Rusch*
This book realistically prepares a singer for life in the world of professional music. Author Gloria Rusch gives candid advice on a wide range of topics and includes extensive interviews with Kevon Edmonds of the group After 7, stage and television producer Ken Kragen, Janis Siegel of Manhattan Transfer, multi-platinum songwriter Andy Goldmark, and other knowledgeable session singers, sound engineers, and arrangers.

_____ 00330349........................................$19.95

### SINGING JAZZ

*The Singers and Their Styles*
by Bruce Crowther
and Mike Pinfold
*Miller Freeman Books*
This book explores the lives, work and music of vocalists past and present to portray the diverse and stimulating world of the jazz singer. Includes: illuminating profiles of legendary artists, including Billie Holiday, Ella Fitzgerald, Sarah Vaughn, Carmen McRae, Louis Armstrong and many more; insights from contemporary masters about the ups and downs of jazz singing today; and A-Z reference section of capsule biographies and essential recording for over 200 singers; a photo section; and lots more.

_____ 00330391...........................................$17.95

### PROFESSIONAL SINGER'S POP/ROCK FAKE BOOK

There's never been such a singer-friendly fake book! Songs include material from the entire rock era, with ballads as well as many up-tempo dance tunes. Over 100 songs every singer needs, in appropriate keys, with intros, interludes, endings and background vocal harmonies – giving singers performable, complete versions of each song. Includes: Beautiful in My Eyes • Blue Suede Shoes • Can You Feel the Love Tonight • Don't Let Me Be Lonely Tonight • Fields of Gold • Great Balls of Fire • Imagine • In My Life • Just the Way You Are • The Loco-Motion • Somewhere Out There • Stand by Me • Tears in Heaven • Time After Time • Twist and Shout • Unchained Melody • Under the Boardwalk • Your Song • and more. Each edition also has songs which are gender-specific.

_____ 00240091 Men's Edition ...................$19.95
_____ 00240090 Women's Edition...............$19.95

### THE SINGER'S MOVIE ANTHOLOGY

*compiled by Richard Walters*
A terrific, unprecedented collection of over 50 songs written for and sung in the movies, with a completely different selection of songs for women and men singers. The songs are presented in the original sheet music editions. Each volume includes historical and plot notes about each movie represented.

### WOMEN'S EDITION

56 songs including: Beauty and the Beast • Isn't It Romantic? • It Might As Well Be Spring • Let Yourself Go • The Man That Got Away • Maybe This Time • On the Good Ship Lollipop • When I Fall in Love • and more.

_____ 00747076 ........................................$19.95

### MEN'S EDITION

55 songs, including: Bella Notte • Easy to Love • I've Got My Love to Keep Me Warm • If I Had a Talking Picture of You • In the Still of the Night • The Way You Look Tonight • When You Wish Upon a Star • and more.

_____ 00747069...........................................$19.95

### STANDARD BALLADS

*Cabaret arrangements for singer and trio (piano, bass, drums) with a companion CD of performances and accompaniments*
Fantastic songs in fantastic renditions, in comfortable keys for pop singing. Contents: All the Things You Are • Autumn Leaves • Call Me Irresponsible • East of the Sun • I Left My Heart in San Francisco • I'll Be Seeing You • In a Sentimental Mood • Isn't It Romantic? • The Very Thought of You • The Way You Look Tonight. Book/CD Packages.

_____ 00740088 Women's Edition .............$19.95
_____ 00740089 Men's Edition ..................$19.95

### 10 POPULAR WEDDING DUETS

*with a companion CD*
10 duets for the wedding. The companion CD contains two performances of each song, one with singers, the other is the orchestrated instrumental track for accompaniment. Contents: All I Ask of You • Annie's Song • Don't Know Much • Endless Love • I Swear • In My Life • Let It Be Me • True Love • Up Where We Belong • When I Fall in Love.

_____ 00740002 Book/CD package.............$19.95

### 10 WEDDING SOLOS

*with a companion CD*
A terrific, useful collection of 10 songs for the wedding, including both popular songs and contemporary Christian material. There are two versions of each song on the companion CD, first with full performances with singers, then with the instrumental accompaniments only. Contents: Here, There and Everywhere • I Swear • The Promise • Someone Like You • Starting Here Starting Now • God Causes All Things to Grow • Parent's Prayer • This Is the Day • Wedding Prayer • Where There Is Love.

_____ 00740004 High Voice Book/CD pkg...$19.95
_____ 00740009 Low Voice Book/CD pkg....$19.95

FOR MORE INFORMATION, SEE YOUR LOCAL MUSIC DEALER, OR WRITE TO:

## HAL•LEONARD® CORPORATION

7777 W. BLUEMOUND RD. P.O. BOX 13819 MILWAUKEE, WI 53213

halinfo@halleonard.com